Charles Brandon Boynton

The Navies of England, France, America and Russia

Being and Extract from a Work on English and French Neutrality and the

Anglo-French Alliance

Charles Brandon Boynton

The Navies of England, France, America and Russia
Being and Extract from a Work on English and French Neutrality and the
Anglo-French Alliance

ISBN/EAN: 9783337167981

Printed in Europe, USA, Canada, Australia, Japan

Cover: Foto ©Andreas Hilbeck / pixelio.de

More available books at **www.hansebooks.com**

OF

ENGLAND, FRANCE, AMERICA, AND RUSSIA,

BEING AN EXTRACT FROM A WORK ON

ENGLISH AND FRENCH NEUTRALITY, AND THE ANGLO-FRENCH ALLIANCE.

BY

Rev. C. B. BOYNTON, D. D.

NEW YORK:
JOHN F. TROW, PRINTER, 50 GREENE STREET.
1865.

THE NAVIES OF ENGLAND, FRANCE, AMERICA AND RUSSIA.

MANY varying newspaper reports of the strength of the navies of Europe have been spread abroad. The following statement of the condition of the English and French navies is copied from the NORTH BRITISH REVIEW for Aug., 1863.

The writer gives the following in a foot-note as his authority : " The figures for England are from a Return to the House of Commons, 1863, No. 30 ; for France, from the official statement for 1862, transmitted by our (the English) ambassador (Parliamentary Pap., 1862, No. 177)."

This table is worthy of especial study. It presents the latest official statement of the actual condition of the English iron-clad navy, and from it we are able to form a correct estimate of the force with which England supposes she can blockade our ports and crush our navy. It shows us exactly the character, the size, form, and armament of her most formidable ships, and in which her power, skill, and science are all concentrated. They are, doubtless, among the most powerful broadside vessels in the world, and, perhaps, would find no equal among ships of that class unless in our own New Ironsides, whose armament is much heavier than theirs. Whether they are a match for our Monitors is a question to be considered.

The opinion of our adversaries, who have been fighting the Monitors for two years with the most formidable ordnance which their British friends could make, is entitled to great weight. The RICHMOND WHIG, in discussing the propriety of submission to England, says : " She has no ships that could encounter the Yankee Monitors with any prospect of success, and although it is easy enough for her to build such, yet they would not be able to cross the ocean. Monitors are made for coast defence and not for ocean navigation. She could not, then, in all probability even break up the blockade of our ports, far less send an army and fleet here to assist us in driving away the Yankees, preparatory to returning to colonial vassalage. We think it, therefore, hardly worth while to inquire into the expediency of returning to the arms of Old England, seeing Old England could not receive us if she would."

The account, we are informed, includes vessels afloat and building :

	Armor-plated.	Liners. Screw.	Frigates. Screw.	Frigates. Paddle.	Corvettes. Screw.	Corvettes. Paddle.	Block-ships, Screw.	Other Steam-ships.	Total Steam.	Total Sailing.
England..............	21	50	44	16	30	....	9	380	566	102
France..............	16	37	29	18	7	9	....	244	360	122

" At Kinburn the French Emperor proved that iron-clad batteries could, without injury, sustain a fire which would be utterly destructive to wooden vessels. He pursued the conclusions thus arrived at, and finally, in 1858, ordered the construction of four iron-plated frigates—La Gloire, L'Invincible, La Normandie, and La Couronne. The first three are on wood frames ; the latter is iron throughout. They are about two hundred and thirty-one feet in length, carrying thirty-six 50-pounders on a single protected deck, with two more on an upper deck, unprotected.* Their engines are of nine hundred horse power, and the crew five hundred and seventy men. All these are at sea, and have been found successful ; but the ports being only about six feet above the water when at load draught, they are placed at a certain disadvantage in bad weather. Subsequently two others, the Solferino and Magenta, were ordered, which have been launched, but are not yet completed. They are armed with a spur ' projecting from the bow, carry their guns in two tiers in the centre of the ship, and the lower ports are eight feet from the water-line. Their length is two hundred and eighty-two feet; draught, twenty-five feet; and horse-power, one thousand.

" In November, 1860, ten more were ordered, which are still on the stocks, and are being slowly proceeded with. They are to be of the Gloire type, and all of wood frames, except the Heroine, which is of iron; but the thickness of the plates has been increased from three and a half to four inches of the Gloire, to four and a half to six inches. All the other iron-plated vessels under construction in France at the present moment are merely floating batteries for harbor defence.

" Our own armor fleet, though more tardily commenced, now stands thus :

	Hull.	Armor-plated.	Tons.	Horse Power.	Length.	Draught.		Guns	Men.
					feet.	feet.	in.		
At Sea.									
Warrior........	Iron	Partially	6,109	1,250	380	22	9	40	704
Black Prince....	"	"	6,109	1,250	380	26	3½	40	704
Defence........	"	"	3,720	600	280	24	11	16	445
Resistance......	"	"	3,710	600	280	24	10	16	455
Royal Oak......	Wood	Wholly	4,056	800	273	25	10½	35	600
Launched.									
Caledonia	Wood	Wholly	4,125	1,000	273	25	10½	35	600
Ocean..........	"	"	4,047	1,000	273	25	10½	35	600
Prince Consort..	"	"	4,045	1,000	273	25	10½	35	600
Hector..........	Iron	Partially.	4,089	800	280	24	8	32	600
Valiant	"	"	4,063	800	280	24	8	32	600
To be Launched 1863.									
Minotaur	Iron	Wholly	6,621	1,350	400	25	8	37	704
Achilles........	"	"	6,079	1,250	380	26	3½	30	704
Royal Alfred....	Wood	"	4,045	800	273	25	10½	35	600
Zealous........	"	Partially	3,716	800	252	25	3	16	....
Royal Sovereign.	"	Wholly	3,963	800	240	22	11	5	200
Prince Albert...	Iron	"	2,529	500	240	20		5	160
Research	Wood	Partially	1,253	200	195	14		4	....
Enterprise......	"	"	990	160	180	14	4½	4	80
To be Launched 1864.									
Agincourt	Iron	Wholly.	6,621	1,350	400	25	8	37	600
Northumberland.	"	"	6,621	1,350	400	25	8	37	600
Favorite	Wood	"	2,186	400	225	20	5	8	160

Other authorities state the number of iron-clads in the French navy at ninety-four; but, as the English reviewer remarks, all but those enumerated are merely swimming batteries for harbor defence, and small gun-boats, such as were used at Kinburn, in the Crimean war. Of these swimming batteries and gun-boats, the NATIONAL ALMANAC for 1863 enumerates seventy-seven, leaving, of the ninety-four iron-clads, only seventeen for the ocean-going ships, which corresponds very nearly to the statement of the REVIEW.

The condition of the Russian navy is said to have been as follows in 1862 :

STEAM VESSELS.	No.
Ships of the line	9
Screw frigates	12
Side-wheel frigates	8
Corvettes	22
Clippers	12
Floating battery (iron-clad)	1
Frigate (iron-clad)	1
Gun-boat (iron-clad)	1
Gun-boats	79
Yachts	2
Schooners	25
Transports	9
Small steamers	68
	249
Sailing vessels	62
	311
Besides these there were, for port service, small vessels	300

Such an enumeration, however, of the ships of any nation presents a very imperfect idea of the strength of its navy. The three hundred small ships here set down are, probably, of no value for offensive purposes, or distant service of any kind ; and the same may be said of hundreds of the thousand vessels of the British navy, or of the seven hundred ships of France.

Since the spring of 1862, Russia has been actively engaged in enlarging her navy, and its effectiveness has been largely increased. Like other nations, she has begun the construction of an iron-clad fleet ; and this, like the American navy, will, it is said, be composed mainly, at first, of ships of the Monitor class, of which many have already been built.

The first necessity of Russia is precisely like our own. She needs batteries which will effectually protect her harbors against the iron-clads of England and France ; and, at one-fourth the cost of such a ship as the Warrior or the Minotaur, she can construct a Monitor battery that would demolish either of these.

Russia, having an unlimited supply of material for a navy, whether timber or iron ; ship-yards so situated that she can defend them against all Europe ; having also the benefit of American experience and skill, is able to construct a navy equal to any in the world ; and, with her new and most valuable possessions on the Pacific, nothing can prevent her from becoming, in the immediate future, a great maritime power.

The Monitor forms of battery will give to Russia, as it does to us, an immense advantage for all purposes of defence. Wherever, in her numerous rivers, she has ten feet of water, she can build a Monitor that will be more than a match for any broadside frigate yet afloat, or that can be floated across an ocean.

Defended by these batteries—invulnerable floating forts as they are—neither America nor Russia can be successfully attacked ; while within this impregnable line of defence they can construct, to say the least, as many, as swift, and as powerful ocean-going ships as any other nation.

But the policy of Russia, like our own, demands peace and self-development, not war and conquest ; and we both need means of defence that will keep our ambitious neighbors at home, and the means on the ocean of defending our growing commerce.

The American navy consists, according to the last report of the Secretary of the Navy, of six hundred and seventy-one vessels, seventy of which are iron-clad. Of the whole number, one hundred and twelve are sailing vessels. The general account of these navies will stand as follows:

	Steam-ships.	Sailing Ships.	Total.
England, ...	566	103	669*
France, ...	360	122	482†
America, ...	559	112	671
Russia (1862), . . .	248	65	313

The NATIONAL ALMANAC says Russia has also four hundred and seventy-four transport and coasting vessels of various kinds, but it does not appear precisely what they are. Russia has also an iron-clad fleet in course of construction, of which no mention is here made. Among her iron-clads are thirteen Monitors of the American pattern, ordered by the emperor after Admiral Lissovsky's report of the trial-trip of the Passaic and of her fifteen-inch guns.

These figures, though copied from official statements, give only approximately the actual number of the ships of these various navies, because changes are being so rapidly made that the statements for 1863 will not apply to the present year. So far as numbers alone are concerned, and including all classes of ships, gun-boats for harbor defence, and floating batteries, these navies may probably be represented in round numbers, with sufficient accuracy, as follows: England,1,000 ships, including all classes; France, 600; America, 700; Russia, 550 to 600.

Numbers alone, however, afford no sufficient data by which the navies of these nations can be compared. Steam has so completely revolutionized navigation and the construction of war ships, that the efficiency of a navy depends, first of all, upon the number of its steam-ships, then upon their speed and size, then upon their character, whether wooden vessels or plated with armor, and, finally, upon the guns with which they are armed. If we compare the steam navies of these four powers, and take the figures for France and Eng-

* Exclusive of small gun-boats and transports; when added, they make 1,014.
† If add swimming batteries and gun-boats, 559.

land from the official statements in the NORTH BRITISH, already quoted, the account stands thus :

English Steam Navy, ...	566
French do. do., ...	360
American do. do., . .	559
Russian (in 1860), ...	242

Since 1860 the Russian steam fleet has been largely increased. A comparison by numbers, though in no case reliable, would approach more nearly to accurate results with the navies of Europe, than in comparing their numbers with ours. The form, size, and armament of the European vessels are so far alike as to enable us to estimate, approximately, their relative strength by a statement of numbers ; but the American navy is so different from all others in the character and armament of its ships, that mere numbers of ships and guns give no true idea of its relative power. For example, the reports state the number of guns in the English navy at about 16,500, while the number in our own is only 4,600 ; but when we remember that twenty-eight of the guns of England's finest frigate, the Warrior, are 68-pounders, and the remaining twelve 100-pounders, while we have many guns on board our ships which carry a shot of 450 pounds, the apparent disparity disappears.

Thus it is seen that a correct opinion of the relative power and efficiency of the American navy can not be formed without a somewhat minute examination of the character and armament of European war ships in comparison with our own. It must be remembered, these comparisons relate to navies and war ships as they are at present. Inventions cannot be monopolized by one nation, and if it appears that our navy and artillery are now, in some important respects, superior to all others, it will depend upon the skill and genius of our countrymen, and the resources of our country, whether this superiority is retained. Judging from the past, however, we have little cause for apprehension. Our mechanics and inventors have never yet failed to protect the country in her hour of need, and we may safely trust them for the future.

In estimating the relative strength of navies, we have now to consider an entirely new element of power, the iron-clad ship; and we must add to this the newly invented heavy artillery. Both these inventions are yet in their infancy, and, astonishing as the results are which are already reached, all estimates must be based upon things as they now are, for no one can foresee how soon our weapons and methods of warfare may be revolutionized again.

The fight between the Merrimac and our wooden frigates, and then between her and the Monitor, closed up one great era in naval warfare. By that battle the wooden navies of the world were virtually annihilated. After that fight the powers of Europe, in calculating their naval force, were reduced to the small catalogue of their iron-clad ships. The London TIMES then said that the navy of England consisted of four ships, and the English statesman was nearly right when he declared, in the House of Commons, that England had no fleet.

In a lecture by J. Scott Russell, Esq., we find the following : " The first question was, were wooden ships worth anything for purposes of warfare ? Sir John C. Hay, the chairman of the committee appointed by Government to make experiments on the effects of artillery upon iron armor, uttered this fatal sentence upon wooden fleets : 'The man who goes into action in a wooden ship is a fool, and the man who sends him there is a villain.' A list of the 'magnificent fleet' which now defends England had been recently published, and it amounted to 1,014 ships of war. This was a very 'formidable inventory,' but he could give them a very simple analysis of the number. Of these 1,014 there were, of wooden ships, 1,010 ; of fast iron ships, 2 ; of slow iron ships, 2. A fleet of twenty Warriors would be more formidable than the whole of the 1,010 wooden ships put together."

This is English opinion of high authority in regard to wooden navies.

It is not intended, by this, to assert that wooden ships are, hereafter, to be considered as absolutely worthless, but they must hold, in the future, nearly the same relation to the iron-clads that merchant vessels have hitherto done to the frigate and the line-of-battle ship. A wooden ship, of any size, may be regarded as absolutely powerless against a properly armored vessel, and, therefore, except as against other wooden ships, or as transports, the immense wooden navies of the world may be left out entirely in our calculations for the future. This destroys, at a blow, the boasted supremacy of England and France, and places England, France, America, and Russia very nearly upon an equality in regard to naval power, with the advantage thus far, however, on the side of the United States, as will be proved.

When a ship like the Merrimac demonstrated in actual battle that she could smash up and send to the bottom a fleet of wooden ships as the mere sport of a day, or, at most, without impairing her fighting powers, it shows, very conclusively, that wooden navies are already a thing of the past, except for certain limited purposes. It is scarcely too much to say that, with the armament which the navies of the world then carried, the Merrimac might have met and sunk every wooden ship on the ocean, with no material damage to herself. She would have destroyed our finest frigates, the Minnesota and the Niagara, as quickly she did the Congress and the Cumberland.

No squadron of wooden vessels can hereafter enter and hold a harbor, or blockade a port, in the presence of a single iron-clad, such as every great naval power has already ; nor could they attack a fort, with any chance of success, under the fire of the new artillery. They may, possibly, pass a fort without material injury, but they would only pass to certain destruction if they were to meet an armored vessel beyond. Laying out of the account, therefore, the wooden navies, in estimating the actual *fighting* power of the nations, the comparison is reduced to the armored vessels now owned in Europe and America, and the power and resources of this and other countries for the construction of war ships hereafter.

The fact that the armor plate for vessels is an American invention, will strengthen our confidence in the skill of our countrymen for the future. As once before, in the style of their frigates and their heavy guns, now again, in the iron shield and form of the ship, Americans have revolutionized the methods of naval war. We may hope, therefore, that she will also lead the nations hereafter. The following account of the invention is copied from the Scientific American for February 7, 1863 :

"On the 22d ult., Senator Cowan, of Pennsylvania, presented a petition in the Senate from A. Stewart and others, asking for a pension to the widow of Thomas Gregg ; it being claimed that he was the original inventor and patentee of iron-clad vessels. This is a new phase of this subject, and a brief history of the invention, according to the information we possess, will, therefore, be of some public interest just now. It is generally admitted by European engineers that, although iron-clad gun-boats were first brought practically into use during the Crimean war, the late Robert L. Stevens and E. A. Stephens, of Hoboken, N. J., were the inventors of them. Vessels protected with angulated iron plates were proposed by them as early as 1816, and, for coast and harbor defence, a description of such vessels was afterwards submitted to a Government board, consisting of Commodores Stewart and Perry and Colonels Thair and Totten, in 1841. It was stated in the document proposing the construction of such a vessel for the defence of New York, that plates of iron four inches in thickness were equal to five feet four inches of oak in resisting a ball at point-blank distance ; and, with the guns then in use, it was supposed that none of their shot could penetrate a vessel clad with such armor. In 1843, a contract was formed between our Government and Messrs. Stevens for the construction of such a floating battery, and $500,000 was furnished by Government, and expended on the battery now at Hoboken.

"During the Crimean war, in 1855, it was found that wooden steam frigates were totally useless in attacking granite casemated forts, defended by big guns firing shells. An application of Stevens's invention was suggested, and several iron-clad gun-boats were then built for the French and English navies. A few of these were employed at the siege of Kinburn, and were decidedly successful. This led the Emperor of France to extend the application of iron plates to one of his large frigates—La Gloire—which was completed three years ago, and was the first regular iron-clad war ship ever built. Since then several have been constructed for the French and English navies—the American invention having thus been first carried into practical use in Europe."

In order to mark the progress of the art of mailing vessels, from the first rude application of the American idea by Louis Napoleon to his gun-boats, at Kinburn, to its present condition, and to exhibit the marked peculiarities of the American iron-clads, it will be instructive to trace the different steps. Passing by the small gun-boats which fought at Kinburn, the first important trial of the iron mail was by the French Emperor on the frigate La Gloire, the construction of which was ordered in 1858. She is simply a frigate of the common model, cased with iron plates about four inches thick. The plates are said to be three and a half inches thick at the stern and bow, and four and a half inches in the centre, covering the ship's battery.

She is described from French authorities as about 257 feet long, carrying thirty-six 50-pounders on a single protected deck. Her engine is of 900-horse power, and her crew consists of 500 men. Her ports are only six feet above the water. Her width is fifty-six feet, and her speed thirteen and a quarter knots per hour. The French Emperor is constructing ten more iron-cased frigates of this class. Besides these, France has now at sea the Normandie, the Invincible, the Couronne, and two larger iron-clad rams, the Solferino and the Magenta. These last carry each fifty-two guns, and have a speed of thirteen and a half knots per hour. The lower ports of these are eight feet above the water. It is also stated by the NORTH BRITISH REVIEW (August, 1863), that these largest French frigates are plated in the centre with iron six inches thick. It may be stated, then, with sufficient accuracy, that Louis Napoleon has at present a fleet of sixteen iron-clad frigates, carrying, each, from thirty-six to fifty-two rifled 50-pounders ; that their armor-plates are some four and a half and some six inches thick, and that they have a speed equal to our fastest war ships, with the exception of some of our small and latest built ships, such as the Eutaw and the Sassacus, being much swifter than any of our own iron-clads.

The Normandie has crossed the Atlantic, but no very favorable account has yet been given of the sea-going qualities of any of these French ships. They are said to roll very heavily, and that their batteries cannot be used in a heavy sea, because the ports roll under. They are also said to be very unhealthy. These are very likely to be objections to all iron-clads, because, when in action, few of them can be properly ventilated, and the same must be true of them in heavy weather. So far as is known, all the broadside iron-plated ships roll heavily in a rough sea, and the remedy for this does not, as yet, appear.

An inspection of the table already copied from the NORTH BRITISH will show that English mailed vessels are, many of them, of much greater size and power than any yet constructed by the French. Nearly all of them are larger than the American Ironsides or Roanoke, and several of them are longer and of greater tonnage than the Dunderberg, our largest iron-clad. A brief description of three of these vessels will enable the reader to compare them with our own iron-plated fleet, and to judge whether we have reason for apprehension should we be compelled to meet them.

The Warrior and the Black Prince are regarded as the model ships of the iron navy of England, and they may be considered as embodying the utmost skill and science of Great Britain at the present time. These ships are 380 feet long ;

their tonnage is 6,000 tons ; their draught is, of the one, 22 feet 9 inches, and of the Black Prince, 26 feet 3 inches. They each carry forty guns : twenty-eight 68-pounder, and twelve 100-pounder Armstrong guns. Their crew is 704 men. Their armor-plates are four and a half inches thick, and the Warrior, on her trial trip, had a speed of fourteen knots, and the Black Prince ran from twelve to thirteen knots per hour. Their engines are of 1,250-horse power.

These ships are only plated with iron for two-thirds of their length, the bow and stern being, as English writers affirm, more vulnerable than a common wooden ship. The battery only is protected by the iron mail, while about sixty feet of the stern and bow are like a common vessel.

The Minotaur is 400 feet long ; her tonnage is 6,621 tons ; her engines are of 1,350-horse power ; her draught is 25 feet 8 inches, and she is to carry thirty-seven guns. Her speed has not been ascertained. Portions of the armor of this ship are said to be six inches thick. The Bellerophon is a newly-devised iron-clad, now being built, whose coming is thus heralded by the London Times : She will be "as terrible an assailant to iron-clads as an iron-clad would be to wooden ships. The object with which this vessel is designed is, in case of another great war, to avoid repetition of the long dreary process of blockading an enemy's fleet, by wearisome and dangerous cruising off the mouth of harbors. The Bellerophon is, in short, to a fleet of iron-clads what a fox-terrier is to a pack of hounds. In case of an enemy's iron fleet running into port, she can follow them with impunity."

But in the description which the Times gives of what it calls " this monster," one fails to discover the immense superiority which is claimed.

She is 300 feet long, 56 feet beam, has a draught of 25 feet, and her tonnage is 4,246 tons. " It is hoped," if certain improvements work well, that she will make fifteen knots per hour ; but she is on the stocks as yet, and her speed is yet to be determined. Her armor-plates are six inches thick, but they reach to the upper deck for only ninety feet of the ship's length ; for the remaining distance of two hundred and ten feet, the plating reaches only six feet above the water, and all above this line and both ends of the vessel are unprotected. She is to be armed with ten broadside guns, of what size we are not informed, and probably that is not yet determined.

The New York TIMES of 22nd February, 1864, has the following notice of the Bellerophon :

"The London TIMES of 22d February admonishes the naval powers of the world that England is now building an armored ship that will be 'as terrible an assailant to iron-clads as an iron-clad would be to wooden ships.' Our contemporary, at a loss for a word that will convey a proper idea of the nature of the new fearful engine of war, calls it a 'monster.' The object, we are told, 'with which this vessel is designed is, in case of another great naval war, to avoid repetition of the long, dreary work of blockading an enemy's fleet by wearisome and dangerous cruising off the mouth of harbors. The Bellerophon (the monster's name) is, in short, to a fleet of iron-clads what a fox-terrier is to a pack of hounds. In case of an enemy's iron fleet running into port, she can follow them with impunity.'

"The confident tone in which the new-comer is heralded would naturally lead to the supposition that some startling principle had been developed in the art of constructing and propelling ships, some new material discovered of greater power to resist projectiles than hitherto known, some new mode of constructing ordnance devised for doubling or quadrupling the present charge of powder. Nothing of the kind —the Bellerophon is simply an iron vessel 300 feet long, 56 feet beam, 25 feet draft, and 4,246 tons burden. Nor does the motive-power to be applied present any remarkable features. 'It is hoped' that by working steam expansively, and by adopting some other modern improvements, to reduce the consumption of coal to $2\frac{1}{4}$ pounds per horse-power per hour. 'If this great result be effected,' says our contemporary, 'she can be depended upon at sea to average 15 knots.' But, as he admits that the Black Prince, which is provided with the best machinery that England could produce a year or two ago, consumes 4½ pounds per horse-power per hour, the hope expressed will scarcely be realized. Thus, neither the size of the terrible ship, nor her speed, present anything extraordinary.

"The 'monster,' therefore, to justify the name, should be absolutely impregnable and carry armament of such weight and disposition as to render opposition hopeless. Fortunately we are not left to conjecture on these points. Everything is described by our contemporary with the utmost exactness. We are told that the impenetrable armor of the Bellerophon is composed of six-inch solid plating backed—we beg our readers not to question our accuracy—backed by nine inches of teak wood attached directly to the thin skin of the iron hull. It was only last week that a six-inch solid plate, manufactured at a celebrated establishment in France, was shot through and broken into fragments at the first discharge from a fifteen-inch gun at Washington Navy Yard. We are aware that the English know nothing of such heavy guns, and that, at Shoeburyness, their trial-ground, guns of fifteen-inch calibre, and their unhandy 450-pound shot, are not to be met with. Small calibres and elongated, handsomely turned projectiles of high initial velocity, are alone tolerated at Shoeburyness—always excepting the wonderful spherical 68-pounder. Velocity is everything at the English official target exhibitions. The shaking of foundations and breaking armor-plates all to pieces at the first discharge with the lumbering fifteen-inch shot, Yankee fashion, has no charm for the scientific artillerists of Shoeburyness. These *savans* delight in noting the gradual extensions of small cracks produced by the impacts of the shot, and their interesting ramifications with other small cracks contiguous to certain bolt-holes. An armor-plate, which at the end of a day's trial exhibits such marks in profusion, is contemplated with much satisfaction. It furnishes matter for interesting speculation on the subject of momentum and cohesive force.

"We have stated the thickness of the Bellerophon's armor

2

—we will now describe how this impenetrable mail is distributed over the ship. Only 90 feet of the entire length is protected by armor reaching the upper deck. The remainder is merely cased by an armor-belt extending six feet above and five feet below water. Above this belt both ends of the ship, for a distance of 210 feet, are composed merely of the ordinary thin plating common to all iron vessels. The quarters of the officers and men are, therefore, wholly unprotected against shot, and may be riddled by transverse or raking fire by guns of any calibre. No provision is made for defending the ends of the ship. Five broadside guns on each side, placed fifteen feet apart, compose her entire armament. A turret vessel of adequate speed may keep close to the stern of the Bellerophon, or lap her sides for sixty feet, without being 'molested by her guns. Let us imagine the Dictator, with her power, to direct her entire battery over the bow, placed as we have stated, how long would the 'monster' endure the raking shot from the fifteen-inch guns which would plow through from end to end ? Bulkheads would avail little against a shot which we have proved can crush a six-inch solid plate into fragments. The unprotected character of the ends of the Bellerophon being admitted, our contemporary observes : 'In action, of course, all the officers and crew would be in the battery, or below the line of the armor.' But where will these officers and men go after the action ? Their quarters, in the meantime, have been utterly demolished by the shells that have riddled the thin skin of the vessel that formed their only protection, and the openings made by the explosion of our fifteen-inch shells, sufficient to admit horse and cart, will, in a seaway, let in such a quantity of water as to defy the power of steam and centrifugal pumps. But we have shown that even the central portion of the Bellerophon which protects her guns is not of sufficient thickness to be proof against shot from our fifteen-inch guns. Let us now consider that in our turret ships of the Dictator and Kalamazoo class, the guns are protected by fifteen inches' thickness, while the hulls are protected by ten inches' thickness of plating and wrought slabs, backed by three and a half feet thickness of oak. We are surprised, under these circumstances, at the absurd pretensions of the London TIMES, and still more to find the British Admiralty, after so many costly experiments, sanction the construction of iron-clads so erroneous in principle as the Bellerophon. Could it be shown that higher speed is attainable on this plan, it might be argued that such a ship can take up her own position and thereby mitigate the evils of erroneous construction ; but so far from the Bellerophon being able to carry a greater amount of motive-power to her tonnage than other ships, her side-armor is twice as heavy as that of our large turreted iron-clads of the Dictator type, which latter, therefore, besides their impregnability, wil carry a greater amount of motive-power, compared with their displacement, than the English ' monster.' "

Of iron-mailed vessels, of the general character described —most of them, however, somewhat smaller—England has between twenty and thirty built, or in process of construction. Like those of France, they are all broadside ships, and, of course, expose an immense surface to an enemy's fire. The importance of this will appear, when they are compared with the American Monitor form of war-ship.

The objections made to the French ships are, that they cannot use their batteries except when the sea is smooth, and that, in rough weather, they roll so as to render them not only uncomfortable, but dangerous. The English ships require from 25 to 26 feet of water, and are, therefore, unable to enter our principal harbors. From their great size, they are unwieldy ; the joints of their armor-plates work in a sea, and leak ; they do not steer safely ; and, from the general tone of English criticisms, one is led to infer that they are by no means satisfied with the performance of the iron fleet. But, as neither the French nor English ships have been, as yet, tested in battle, no very definite opinion of their qualities can be formed.

We know, however, exactly the effect which certain kinds of artillery will produce upon iron plates, such as those which form their armor ; and as the American ships have been exposed, at short range, to the heaviest cannon and the most destructive shot which England could furnish to the rebels, while at the same time our guns have been tried upon armor-plates in action, we have the means of forming a very accurate opinion of our power for attack or defence, as compared with other nations.

The condition and character of the American navy demands a separate chapter, and this will involve, also, a description of our artillery, and then all will be able to make the proper comparison between our navy and those of Europe.

THE AMERICAN NAVY.

At the commencement of Mr. Lincoln's administration our navy consisted of only forty-six vessels. In December, 1864, it numbered 671 vessels, mounted with 4,610 guns. The aggregate tonnage of these ships was about 510,000 tons.

The creation of such a navy in so short a time, considering the number and character of the vessels, is without a parallel in the history of war. It is at once a most cheering proof of the vast resources of our country, and of the wisdom and energy with which our Navy Department has been conducted. In the brief space between the breaking out of the war and December, 1864, the country has been elevated into a first-class naval power ; and, probably, those who have been disposed to criticise the operations of the Secretary would find it very difficult to point out a course by which the safety and honor of the country would have been more securely guarded.

It is no small proof of ability in the management of the navy, that there was skill enough to provide, and independence enough to use, a form of war-ship and a kind of cannon before untried, but which time and experience have shown were alone, of all ships and weapons then known, capable of meeting the emergency.

Had there been a frigate built like the Warrior in Hampton Roads at the time of the appearance of the Merrimac, and armed with the Warrior's guns, there are good reasons for believing that she would have been overmatched by the rebel ship. The Merrimac, with her heavy armament and her sloping armor, could not, probably, *at that time*, have been beaten by any ship afloat, except the Monitor. The Monitors and the fifteen-inch guns have rendered the creation of a rebel navy impossible, and these alone could have done it ; and this is a sufficient answer to all by whom they have been condemned.

This subject, however, will be more fully discussed in another place. The American navy is an original creation. In the forms of its most powerful ships, and the character of its armament, it is unlike every other.

A thorough study of all the other navies of the world would give no data from which to judge of the efficiency of the American vessels. One would be entirely deceived by counting their guns, or estimating their length, breadth, and tonnage, or the number of their crews. These things alone do not inform us whether they are superior or inferior to the war-ships of other nations. They are modelled after new and strictly American ideas. Whether good or bad, they belong entirely to this new world. They are creations of this Western Republic. Not alone our Monitors, but our other ships, are American in their fitting up, and in the character of their weapons. Judged by the old standards, nothing is more deceitful. An American ship of two guns, of the latest model, may, perhaps, prove a match for a common forty-gun frigate ; and it is very certain that we have two-gun vessels, one of which might destroy the whole fleet with which Nelson fought. It is necessary, then, to know both the character and the armament of our war-vessels before we can judge of their efficiency. The following statements will furnish the necessary information :

It will, probably, not be denied that, up to the time of the invention of armor-clad vessels, the Americans had been the teachers of the nations in the art of ship-building, whether sail or steam vessels, whether for commerce or for war. Great length, as compared with tonnage, sharpness of bow, and speed, were characteristics of American ships and steamboats. It is not deemed exaggeration that American genius has revolutionized naval architecture, and that the speed of European ships has been obtained by following, in the main, the model of the vessels of the United States. The ocean tub has been displaced everywhere by the long, graceful structure, which first of all bore the Stripes and Stars. The London Times sneered at the Niagara when she went over to aid in laying the Atlantic cable ; but the finest frigates and corvettes which England has since built have assumed the Yankee form, and their boasted Warrior appears like a Niagara somewhat magnified.

A writer in an English quarterly boasts that the British ocean mail-steamers have driven the American ones from the seas ; but he forgets to state that the Collins line furnished the model for her ships, and that the American line failed only because, in a new enterprise, and one so expensive, private capital could not contend against the patronage of the British government.

Had our government given a liberal and steady support to our own vessels, there would have been a different result. The fact that our steamers have obtained a speed of twenty-five miles per hour upon the Hudson ; that some of our lake-vessels have made twenty-two miles per hour for hours together—such steamships as the Vanderbilt and those of the California line ; and the fact that our new war-steamers overhaul the swiftest steamers that our English friends have built to run the blockade ; these things do not indicate that we shall be very soon driven from the ocean by the superiority of the vessels of other nations.

Such of our iron-clads as are yet afloat lack speed, but the main idea in their construction was invulnerability ; and the event has shown, that if this had been sacrificed to speed or any other quality, it would have been fatal to our navy and our country's cause.

There is great reason to be thankful that those at the head of our navy were wise enough, in the first experiment upon which our all depended, to construct ships which no artillery of the enemy could penetrate ; for upon that single question the destiny of the country was at that moment hung.

The best and most destructive projectiles of Europe were hurled against our ships at Charleston, and Europe was watching earnestly the result. It would inform England and France whether intervention would be safe.

The only armored vessel of the common form which attacked Fort Darling was ruined by ten-inch shot ; and the only Monitor-shaped ship in which speed was aimed at in the construction, was riddled and sunk at Charleston.

Had all our vessels at Charleston been as vulnerable as the Keokuk, the rebel cause would have triumphed at home and abroad, though our fleet had been the swiftest on the ocean.

Four distinct eras appear in the creation of our navy. In one of these we followed the European models, and failed to produce an effective ship. The distinctive American idea has controlled the other three—the placing the heaviest possible armament in the smallest possible space—thus diminishing the size of the ship in proportion to her armament, presenting a smaller surface to an enemy's shot, and lessening the number of the crew. If to this is added the American idea of a heavy shot with a low velocity, rather than a small one with greater velocity, the idea of a *smashing* projectile rather than a penetrating one, the reader will have the leading principles which have governed the construction of the American navy and the manufacture of American cannon. Through various steps and countless experiments, these ideas have led to the Monitors and the fifteen-inch and twenty-inch guns, while, at the same time, every effort has been made to perfect our rifled cannon.

The ships with which the Americans won their first naval renown, in the war of 1812–'15, were constructed with the intention of bringing the armament of a line-of-battle ship

within the limits of a frigate. This was so nearly accomplished as to fill England with astonishment and alarm. It
was found that the registered rate of our vessels by no means
indicated their actual power ; and the result was, that when
the Guerriere, a British forty-four-gun frigate, was laid along-
side the Constitution, an American forty-four, the English
frigate was demolished in fifteen minutes. Similar results
followed, as is well known, in other actions ; and though it
was conceded that the rapidity of the American fire was
generally greater than that of the English, still our almost
unbroken success was probably mainly due to the superior
weight of the American broadside. The manner in which the
American idea of a heavy armament was carried out, will
appear from the following comparison between British and
American ships which fought in the war of 1812-'15. The
figures rest upon the authority of "James's Naval History,"
and "Cooper," as quoted by Mr. Alison. The weight of the
broadside is thus stated :

American frigate Constitution,	.	768 lbs.
American frigate United States, .		. 864 lbs.
British frigate Guerriere,	.	517 lbs.
British frigate Macedonian, .	.	. 528 lbs.

The advantage thus gained was decisive, and the results
gave an *éclat* and character to the American navy which it
has never lost. It was the first triumph of American sagacity
on the ocean, and it has shaped since their whole naval
policy. The character of the American frigate of that period
will more fully appear from another comparison. The NORTH
BRITISH, for August, 1863, states, upon the authority of
"James's Naval History," the broadside of a hundred-gun
ship—the three-decker, such as Nelson fought with—at
1,260 lbs.

The broadside of the United States frigate was 864 lbs.,
more than two-thirds of that of the English line-of-battle
ship with her one hundred guns.

The American and English ideas will appear still more
strongly contrasted by another statement. According to the

NORTH BRITISH, in the article alluded to, the English ship-of-the-line in the beginning of this century, in the time of Nelson, averaged about 2,000 tons' burden, and her broadside weighed 1,260 lbs. Now the Warrior's tonnage is more than 6,000 tons, and the weight of her broadside is no more than 1,612 lbs. The American frigate Minnesota is of 3,300 tons' burden, but the weight of her broadside is about 2,500 lbs.

One of our sloops, like the Brooklyn, throws a broadside equal in weight, and far more than equal in efficiency, to that of the old English hundred-gun ship. The difference between a British and American ship is again illustrated by the American New Ironsides and the English Warrior, both iron-clads, and representative ships. The American frigate is 3,400 tons' burden, the Warrior a little more than 6,000 tons. The American ship throws a broadside about equal in weight to that of the British vessel, which is nearly double her size ; and to make the American idea stand forth more prominent, the new Ironsides mounts only eighteen guns, while the Warrior carries forty.

Again : the turreted frigate Roanoke throws from her *six* guns a weight of metal, at a broadside, almost equal to that of the Warrior when using twenty guns on a side ; and, if armed with six fifteen-inch guns, as she can be if needed, her broadside from these six cannon would exceed that of the Warrior's guns by at least one thousand pounds.

These facts present, very clearly, the peculiarities of American ships and American artillery, and the difference between them and the vessels and cannon of Europe. They show that the American mind is not working at random in regard to our weapons of war, but in accordance with original and clearly-defined ideas. The second era in the construction of the United States navy began after the war of 1812-'15, in which an effort was made to follow the European model of the three-deck line-of-battle ship. It resulted in those failures which are now used for receiving-ships, such as the Ohio, the North Carolina, the Pennsylvania, and the

Vermont, which are utterly worthless, except as a sort of floating warehouse. The American mind does not work successfully in European harness. In the third era there was a return to the American idea, and it produced such frigates as the Minnesota, the Wabash, the Merrimac, the Roanoke, and the Niagara. They were by no means perfect ships. They failed in speed ; but still they were the most formidable frigates afloat. The direction which American improvement has taken is indicated by the Minnesota, whose battery of fifty guns throws more than twice the weight of shot, at a broadside, than was thrown by the hundred-gun ship of Nelson's time, while the British Warrior, three times the size of the old three-decker, uses less than 400 lbs. more shot than the " old liner " in a broadside.

The French and English hundred and hundred-and-twenty-gun ships, that were fought at Trafalgar and the Nile, would be greatly overmatched by such a frigate as the Minnesota, with her heavy guns, and firing shell horizontally, as the Russians did at Sinope, and by which the Turkish fleet was destroyed.

The fourth era in the creation of the navy of the United States has been marked by the introduction of three new classes of ships : the swift, heavily-armed, wooden corvette, such as the Lackawanna, the Canandaigua, and the Sacramento ; the still swifter, double-bowed steamers, like the Sassacus and the Eutaw ; and the various forms of iron-clads, of which the Monitors are the most numerous. This period has also been distinguished by a new form of American cannon ; and these new ships and this new artillery have, it is believed, revolutionized the art of war, both by sea and land. The reasons for such a belief will appear from what follows. As has been stated in a previous chapter, France and England began the construction of iron-clad vessels soon after the close of the Crimean war—France in 1858, and England somewhat later. The general character of these ships has been already described. The rebel leaders, in preparing for rebellion, had made themselves familiar with these operations in Europe, and, almost immediately after the war had begun, turned their attention to the preparation of a formidable iron-clad ship.

They had seized the most important navy-yard of the country—that of Norfolk—though not before the vessels lying there had been scuttled or set on fire and sunk. Among these was the frigate Merrimac, of the class of the Minnesota, of about 3,200 tons' burden. This ship the Confederates soon raised, and proceeded to convert her into an ironclad battery and ram. In size she was about equal to the New Ironsides, to which ship she bore some general external resemblance. There was nothing original in her construction. Her armor formed an angle with her sides, covering her deck and guns after the manner of a roof, according to a plan which had been proposed but not adopted in England, at least in her first-class vessels.

In the absence of official information, the exact form and thickness of her armor cannot be stated. It has been variously described, some believing it to have been formed of railroad iron, and others stating that she was mailed with plates, four inches or four and a half inches in thickness. One important test was, however, applied, which showed more conclusively her powers of resistance than any measuring the thickness of iron plates could have done. She was attacked with nine-inch, ten-inch, and eleven-inch guns, their shot weighing, respectively, about 100 lbs., 128 lbs., and 169 lbs. The heaviest guns of the Minnesota, the Cumberland, and the Congress made no impression upon her, and, although the Monitor engaged her for five hours with eleven-inch guns, and, at times, only a few yards from her side, it is not known, certainly, that her armor was once penetrated, although compelled to haul off and signal for assistance, her hull shattered by the smashing power of the heavy shot that yet did not pass through her armor. This proves that she was a vessel of the most formidable character, and that her mail was equal in resisting shot to that of any French or English vessel which had then been built. Her destructive power was sufficiently shown, by her shattering and sinking, in a few minutes, with perfect ease, and with not the slightest inconvenience to herself, so far as is known, two heavily-armed wooden ships. She destroyed them as readily as if they had been bark canoes, and no one doubts that the Minnesota would have shared the same fate, had the Merrimac been suffered to approach her. The wooden navies of the world were virtually sunk with the Congress and Cumberland, and from that time it was evident that the ships which were to rule the seas in future were yet to be built. The ocean-sceptre of Britian was broken by the blow which crushed in the sides of the Cumberland, and all nations were to start anew in the creation of navies. England, said the Times, had but two ships.

The morning after the destruction of the Congress and Cumberland was the most hopeful one, and the proudest one, that ever rose on the slaveholding Confederacy. They seemed to have a war-engine capable of destroying with ease the whole American navy, and of entering any harbor, of capturing or burning all our sea-coast cities. If the Merrimac was indeed a sea-boat, all this was really within reach of the rebels, so far as then was known. It is believed that nothing could have prevented her, if opposed only by our wooden ships, or our forts as they then were, from reaching Washington, Philadelphia, or New York.

Had she succeeded in this, it probably is not too much to say, that the cause of the Union would have been lost. The Christians of the country will never cease to believe that it was the special interposition of God which brought the Monitor to the scene of action just in the hour of the country's greatest need, and put an end to the career of the sea-giant which threatened to crush us at a blow.

The Merrimac had settled, conclusively, the helplessness of a wooden ship, or squadron of ships, when attacked by an iron-clad. This was a mailed ship, patterned in general after the European model, differing mainly in her sloping armor; but the next day she was met by a war-ship such as the world never saw before, a fresh invention of the genius of the West, a hurried, rough, imperfect embodying of an idea destined to work another revolution in the structure of ships and the methods of naval war. The reader should remember the size of the Merrimac in order to judge correctly the combat which followed. Her tonnage was more than twice as great as that of the frigates Constitution and United States, with which the victories of 1812–'15 were won, and almost twice as great as that of the hundred-gun ships of the time of Nelson. She ranked with the most formidable iron-clads of Europe, for she was completely mailed, and her angulated armor was thought to give her an advantage even over these.

The next morning after the terrible feat with which she had startled the country, she came forth for the purpose of destroying the Minnesota, and then she intended, as was thought, to proceed at once to Washington and the Northern cities.

As she approached the Minnesota, her progress was interrupted by a strange-looking *something*, no one on board the frigate knew what. " A cheese-box on a raft," they called the queer little boat, raft, or canoe, or whatever it might be. The huge, mailed monster seemed at first disposed to take no notice of this diminutive craft, and steered for the Minnesota. But the first shot from her small adversary· was a startling proof of power.

The practised ear was taught by that report that the new-comer had at least one formidable gun. The Merrimac stopped her engines and paused to observe her little enemy· It came straight on, showing no sign of fear, indicating a wish to come at once to close action. The first shot which struck the Merrimac showed her officers that the Monitor was throwing projectiles of unusual weight, and created some anxiety, which was by no means lessened when they found that their own broadside made no impression upon the little turret, which hurled forth shot·in return, whose stroke made the huge ship shudder. Fearing for the result, at length, the Merrimac undertook to do what many think so easily done—to run the Monitor down and sink her. She failed, but in the attempt exposed herself more than before to the Monitor's shot, while the Monitor was uninjured. This first battle of the iron-clads continued for five hours, and then the Merrimac, apparently much injured, drew off, signaled for aid, and was accompanied by some steam-tugs back to Norfolk. This was the end of her career. She was shortly after blown up, rather than risk her in another action.

In its bearings upon naval war, the structure of war-ships, and the destinies of this country and Europe, this may be considered the most important naval battle of modern times. The ships engaged in it so far represented the navies of the world, that safe general inferences could be drawn from it in regard to the future.

The wooden navies of Europe and the United States were virtually on trial there, through the Minnesota, the Cumberland, and the Congress. The iron-clads of France and England were so nearly represented by the Merrimac, that an opinion formed of her would equally apply to them with very little modification ; while the Monitor presented the rude germ of the turreted navy which the United States has constructed since.

The result was, that while the wooden ships were as egg-shells before the iron-plated one, the little turreted vessel, with her two heavy guns, defeated and drove off, with no injury to herself, a first-class iron-clad broadside frigate, armed with the heaviest guns then known to European war.

This combat not only saved our own navy and our cause, but it prevented the rebels from constructing one, by destroying the basis of it ; and showed England and France that the Americans could build a ship in three months which would be a formidable antagonist for their most powerful frigates. To suppose that this fact had no bearing upon their policy, is to believe them less prudent than usual. The Monitor did, indeed, admonish Europe that intervention would be dangerous. Persistent efforts are made to show that the Monitors are all inefficient, an almost worthless class of ships, not worthy to be compared with the broadside frigates of England and France, and that the Government is merely wasting the people's money in their construction.

Before entering into a particular discussion of the peculiarities, merits, and defects of the Monitors, it may be well to offer a few suggestions in regard to this now famous battle in Hampton Roads. First, let it be asked, How would that fight have terminated had the Merrimac encountered, instead of the Monitor, a frigate the exact counterpart of the English Warrior? The Merrimac was plated, it is said, all round; the Warrior only for two-thirds of her length. Considering the terrible effect of the shells of the Merrimac upon the Congress and Cumberland, "converting them," as an English reviewer says, "into helpless, burning charnel-houses," how would the Warrior-built frigate have escaped a similar shattering in her unprotected bow and stern? The Warrior is armed with 68-pounder smooth-bores and twelve 100-pounder Armstrong rifles. The batteries of the Cumberland and Minnesota threw heavier shot than these, and made no impression upon the Merrimac; while the shot of the Monitor weighed 169 pounds, and, by some statements, 180 pounds, and these were fired often at the shortest possible range, and yet it is not known that the frigate's armor was pierced.

What reason is there, then, for supposing that such a ship as the Warrior could have seriously injured the Merrimac? and how much reason we have, on the contrary, to think that the rebel frigate would, with her heavier armament and shell-guns, have been victorious!

Our own broadside frigate, the New Ironsides, armed as she now is, would, in all probability, capture or destroy such a ship as the Merrimac; but it would be with far greater risk than was run by the Monitor, because her ends, like those of the Warrior, are not protected by armor. At Charleston, shells pierced these unshielded parts at the distance of a mile; and, in close action with the Merrimac, she might, perhaps, have been seriously injured, or destroyed even, by her shells. The conclusion seems inevitable, that, for the purpose intended, the little Monitor was better adapted than any other ship then afloat.

Indeed, it is very doubtful whether any other vessel then in existence could have stopped and driven back into Norfolk this formidable iron-clad of the rebels. But suppose that one of the new Monitors had encountered the Merrimac with fifteen-inch instead of eleven-inch guns. It is now known, both from the fate of the Atlanta and subsequent experiments, that a few minutes would have sufficed to disable the frigate. While the eleven-inch shot did not pierce the Atlanta's armor, the fifteen-inch gun sent its shot crashing through, and with such a shock, that the crew of the rebel ship could not be brought back to their guns.

It is not, then, exaggeration to say, as the Charleston correspondent of the London TIMES has done, that the Americans, since the rebellion broke out, have twice revolutionized the art of war—once on the sea, with the Monitors and their enormous guns ; and once on the land, with their new rifled artillery.

The invention of the Monitor form of war-vessel and the heavy cannon have saved the country, at least for the present, from intervention and foreign war ; for they have rendered it certain that no ship known, that can cross the ocean, could withstand an attack from our small Monitors even, armed with fifteen-inch guns, or our heaviest rifled one. Experiments already made leave no doubt on this point.

The extraordinary performance of the small nondescript craft, that saved from destruction our finest wooden frigate, and beat off the first iron-clad frigate that ever went into action, determined the Government to rely mainly upon this class of ship for the present defence of our harbors, and for the reduction of the sea-coast fortifications in the hands of rebels. As large sums of money have been spent upon this new fleet, and as severe censure has been cast upon the Navy Department on this account, it is important that Americans should fully understand what the peculiarities are of those ships which the Government has made so prominent in the creation of our navy.

It will be seen that Mr. Ericsson, in his Monitor ship, has aimed, first, to carry out the American idea of the heaviest possible battery in the smallest possible space ; and then to construct an iron-clad vessel with the least possible space exposed to the enemy's shot, and so render it invulnerable by thicker armor than a broadside ship can carry. As an example, the side-armor of the Dictator is eleven inches thick, and her turret is fifteen inches thick. She is, consequently, invulnerable to any shot yet known, but no broadside ship could swim a moment cased all round with such an armor as that. Mr. Ericsson then places two heavy guns in a revolving turret, whose walls, in the first Monitor, were nine inches thick. This turret is placed upon an open deck, so that the guns, as the turret revolves, can be fired in any direction. This deck is sunk almost to a level with the water ; and the small space above the water-line can be so heavily armored as to be impenetrable, without destroying the buoyancy of the ship. In action, then, the Monitor ship presents a very small mark to an enemy's guns—only her turret, nine feet high, and some twenty or twenty-two feet in diameter, and a very narrow line of her side, just at the water's edge. These ships, in addition to the battle with the Merrimac, have been exposed, at short range, to the heaviest artillery and steel-shot at Charleston, and no shot has yet penetrated either a turret or a side. That they should be injured by a fire which would have sunk any other ship afloat, was a matter of course ; but no gun, rifled or smooth-bore, which the rebels yet have tried, with all the skill of England at their disposal, has sent a shot through a turret or the side of a Monitor.

Plates have been cracked and bent, but, with the exception of two or three casualties from bolt-heads, (now guarded against,) the Monitors have protected their crews from shot under a fire which no other vessels were ever exposed to, and which there is no reason to believe any other ships afloat could endure.

In the creation of a new navy, the Government has constructed—or is building, at least—four classes of Monitors,

besides other forms of iron-clad vessels, both for ocean service
and for our rivers. A brief description of one of each kind
will enable the reader to judge of the present efficiency and
probable future of the American iron-clads; and this, with
an account of our new wooden ships, will show what claim
we have to be considered a first-class naval power, and
whether we shall be able hereafter to defend our commerce
abroad and our cities at home.

The small Monitor which encountered and beat the Merrimac, the pioneer ship of her class, was truly an *extempore*
vessel, hurriedly built, to meet the emergency which the
rebels were preparing for the country at Norfolk; and the
great value of the principles upon which she was constructed
is shown in the victory which was won over so formidable an
adversary.

The following facts in regard to the Monitors are derived
from an article in the SCIENTIFIC AMERICAN, one of the best
authorities upon such subjects in this or any other country.
The dimensions of the original Monitor were as follows :

Extreme length on deck, over the armor, . .	173 feet.
Extreme beam on deck, over the armor,	41 feet 6 inches.
Depth, ...	12 feet.
Length of iron hull, .	127 feet.
Width of iron hull, . .	36 feet 2 inches.
Projection of armor-shelf forward, .	14 feet.
Projection of armor-shelf aft, . . .	32 feet.

The thickness of the side-armor was five inches above
the water-line, diminishing first to four inches, and finally to
three inches below the water. The whole armor above the
water was two feet three inches of wood, and five inches of
iron. The turret was made of eight thicknesses of one-inch
iron plates. Its inside diameter was twenty feet, and its
height nine feet. Her armament was two eleven-inch guns,
laid side by side, and they revolved with the turret. Such
was the diminutive affair which conquered a first-class iron-
clad broadside frigate. Her success was due to three things ;
the invulnerable turret which shielded her guns and crew, the

great weight of her shot, and the extremely small surface—little more than her turret—exposed to the enemy's shot. Her defects were many, but they did not affect the main principles of her construction. She was slow, but there is no good reason why a vessel built on the Monitor principle should not be a swift one, and the Puritan and Dictator are expected to be very fast.

Notwithstanding her faults, she had settled the value of the principles of her construction, and the Government at once determined to build nine more according to the general plan, with such changes as experience had suggested. The nine vessels of this new Monitor fleet were modelled alike, and their dimensions are as follows :

Length on deck,	200 feet.
Width on deck,	45 feet.
Depth on deck,	12 feet.
Length of hull proper,	159 feet.
Width of hull proper,	37 feet 8 inches.
Overhang of armor-shelf forward,	16 feet.
Overhang of armor-shelf aft,	25 feet.
Tonnage	844 tons.
Draught of water,	10 feet.

The side-armor is composed of five one-inch plates. The thickness of the armor and its wood backing is three feet eight inches. The deck is plated with two thicknesses of half-inch iron. The turret is eleven inches thick, made of eleven plates one inch thick. It is nine feet high, and the inside diameter is twenty feet. The armament was originally intended to be two fifteen-inch guns. But this now varies : some carry one fifteen-inch gun and one eleven-inch gun, and others one fifteen-inch smooth-bore, and one Parrot rifle, a 150 or 200-pounder. These are the ships which were engaged at Charleston.

Still another fleet of nine are, at this time, nearly all ready for use. They vary little from those last described, except that they are about one-fourth larger, being about 225 feet long, and of about 1,000 tons' burden. The projection of the armor-shelf is less, and the vessels have greater speed, and have proved to be good and safe sea-boats.

Admiral Porter's report of the admirable qualities of the Monitors exhibited during the severe gale off Wilmington, has set at rest all doubt as to the seaworthiness of this class of vessels.

In addition to these, some twenty Monitors of less draught are under way, which, in other respects, are similar to the last described, being 225 feet long, and 25 feet wide. They are intended to be fast boats.

Besides these, there is another class of Monitor ships, now nearly finished, differing, in some particulars, from those already mentioned. They are much larger, some of them being nearly 1,600 tons' burden. Their side-armor is ten inches thick, and the thickness of the turrets is fifteen inches. Some of these have two turrets.

In the frigate Roanoke there is a combination of the turreted and the broadside ship. She is of the same class as the Merrimac. Her upper works were taken off, her sides plated all round with iron four and five-eighths inches thick in the central portion of the ship, and somewhat thinner, as is stated, at the bow and stern. Upon her deck are placed three revolving turrets, of the Ericsson form ; and in these she carries six guns—two fifteen-inch, two eleven-inch, and two 150-pounder rifles. The weight of her broadside, as at present armed, is about 1,500 pounds. But she can carry six fifteen-inch guns if necessary, and then the weight of her broadside would be about 2,500 pounds. She is said to be a slow ship, and it seems not probable that her peculiar form will be adopted in the construction of new vessels, although she has never been tried in action.

The Dictator and the Puritan represent still another class of Monitors, which are intended to be swift sea-going ships ; and, if successful—of which no doubt is entertained, except in regard to their speed—they will be the most formidable ships of our navy, and absolutely invulnerable to any artillery yet in service in Europe. These two ships are so nearly alike, in general form and construction, that a description of the Dictator, principally copied from the New York TRIBUNE, will answer for the Puritan, except that the Puritan is twenty-one feet longer than the Dictator, and will have two turrets. In other respects, the ships are, in general, alike.

It having been frequently stated that the Dictator is an ocean iron-clad, the impression prevails that she resembles the New Ironsides and other vessels built for the purpose of going to sea. This is not so. The Dictator has none of the paraphernalia of such ocean-vessels as we are in the habit of looking at in our harbors. She has none of the tall bulwarks, no masts, no rigging, no capstan on deck—nothing, in fact, that looks like an ordinary ship. A long-armed man could dip his hands into the water from her deck.

The dimensions of the hull of the vessel are as follows : Extreme length over all, 314 feet. The aft overhang being thirty-one feet, and forward overhang thirteen, it leaves 270 feet between perpendiculars,—extreme breadth fifty, and depth twenty-two and a half feet. Like the original Monitor, and the Monitors that are now in course of construction, the Dictator is almost exclusively iron—her frames, kelsons, and plating, being of that metal. A person looking at her in the river can form no idea of her appearance when she is completely out of the water. If an ordinary ship were lifted up, and an immense shelf of eleven feet of iron placed on the top of her deck, overhanging for a space of some four feet on each side, she would resemble the Dictator. Taking into account the curvature of the sea, the Dictator could not be seen four miles off.

The armor of the original Monitor consisted of five inches of iron, laid on in single plates, each one inch thick. That of the Warrior consisted of four and a half inches of iron, laid on in a solid slab like our own iron-clad frigate Roanoke. The French frigate La Gloire had also four and a half inches of iron laid on in a solid slab. Now, the Dictator has on her sides eleven inches of iron, and five inches of this is in solid beams, somewhat like the Warrior, the La Gloire, and the

Roanoke, except that the plates of the latter were in very large slabs, while those of the Dictator are in beams five by eight inches. Over these five-inch blocks of iron are six one-inch plates of iron ; making altogether an armor of eleven inches of iron, the same dimensions as the armor of a turret of the Passaic, Montauk, etc. The armor begins at the deck and goes down six feet, which takes it about four feet below the water ; so that the deck of the ocean iron-clad Dictator will only be about two feet over water. Below this armor there are sixteen feet of the ship, composed of plating 13-16 of an inch thick. The weight of the armor is about five hundred tons—the burden of a pretty large sized steamer.

There will be but one turret, of an improved pattern. It was originally intended to cover it with twenty-four inches of iron, but the perfection to which its construction has now been brought will render fifteen inches sufficient. This is four inches more than the armor of the Passaic class of turret, and ten inches more than the armored sides of those vessels. The apparatus for working the guns will be more perfect than any yet carried out. The revolution in naval artillery, caused by the facility with which four or five men can work the fifteen-inch gun, will be made still more startling when one or two men can handle such immense pieces of ordnance. The gear of the turret is different from that of the other vessels only in point of size. The turret complete will weigh almost five hundred tons, or thereabouts, being as heavy, almost, as the entire armor of the vessel.

The ram is almost the finest piece of work aboard the ship. The ram proper is twenty-two feet of solid oak and iron ; unlike the Keokuk, which protruded from the bottom of the hull near the keel, this extends from the top of the deck, being, as it were, an extension of the entire armor of the ship. Another advantage in this ram is, that it could be carried away without any material damage or injury to the vessel, and without her making water.

The decks are perfectly clear of all incumbrances except the turret. The same objection made to the other Monitors, relative to their liability to be injured by plunging shot from forts, is valid in the Dictator's case ; but it is only just to say, that, of the iron-clad vessels engaged in the attack on Charleston, none has suffered any serious inconvenience from injuries done to the deck. It seems almost impossible, and has proved so, that a projectile- fired from a ship could enter the deck. The armor of the deck consists of one and a half inches of iron, laid on in two plates, in the same manner as in the other vessels.

The berth-deck—that on which the crew and officers are to live—is a very commodious one, the head-room being equal to that of any first-class sailing frigate in the navy. A man six feet high, with his hat on, can walk, without stooping, from end to end of it.

The ship is ventilated by three immense blowers ; two for the use of the vessel generally, and one for the express purpose of ventilating the engine-room. These blowers are of immense size, about seventy-two inches by forty-eight inches. An air-trunk, supplying a blower eight feet in diameter, is placed thirty-five feet from the stern. The air to supply the other blowers is drawn from the top of the turret and distributed through the ship.

The machinery of the Dictator is of greater power than that of any man-of-war built in this country or in Europe. The cylinders are one hundred inches in diameter. Cylinders of these dimensions have never been built in this city, except for side-wheel steamboats. The cylinders are bolted to massive wrought-iron kelsons, ten feet deep, and some twenty-four inches in width. They are both in line, athwart ships, and have large slide and expansive valves, the latter working over the former. A peculiar feature of the machinery is the absence of guides, cross-heads, and other cumbrous parts. The piston, four feet stroke, has a trunk attached to it. The boilers are immense, six in number, and have fifty-six furnaces, and an aggregate grate-surface of 1,100 feet ; allowing twelve pounds of coal per square foot of grate-surface, the vessel will require at least one hundred and forty tons of coal

per day of twenty-four hours' steaming at full speed, which
will never be requisite excepting when chasing an enemy.
The weight of these boilers will be almost seventy tons each,
that is, four hundred and twenty tons altogether, without
water ; so that when they are completed they will weigh over
seven hundred tons. The propeller shaft is a gigantic piece
of forge-work ; it weighs something like thirty-six tons, the
burden of an average sloop. The propeller is a right-handed
true-screw, twenty-one and a half feet in diameter ; has
thirty-four feet pitch, and weighs 39,000 pounds. There is
no outboard bearing for the shaft. What piston-speed will
be obtained from the engines remains to be seen. The propeller cannot be injured by any projectile, as a shot would
have to pass through twenty-six feet of water to strike it.
The engines are calculated to be something in the neighbor-
hood of 5,000-horse-power.

One of the greatest difficulties in the way of making
the iron-clads permanently useful was that of protecting the
bottoms from the filth which concentrated there and prevented them from moving. The original Monitor had to be
towed from Fortress Monroe to Washington, on account of
her bottoms being so foul. The English frigate Warrior
also experienced a similar inconvenience. All sorts of paints
have been tried, and all with want of success. The most
popular was a sort of English "peacock" paint, which was
used in some of the mail-steamers ; but it did very little
good. On the bottom of the Dictator, however, and on
all of our iron-clads to be built henceforward, and most
of the naval-built vessels, a successful remedy has been
devised, which will keep the bottoms perfectly clear of all
filth. It is called "ship-zinc" paint, and is perfectly white
in color. Some thirty years since a vessel was coated with it
in England ; she arrived here a few weeks ago, and her bottoms were found in perfect order. The government has
responsible parties furnishing the paint, and its purity can be
relied on. It is confidently expected that a vessel so complete, with eleven inches of armor and such a heavy battery
will prove herself the Dictator of the ocean.

"Capt. Tyler, of the Royal Engineers, in a lecture before the United Service Institution, Jan. 18th, delighted his hearers by assuring them that 'the turrets of the monitors and their port-stoppers were effective principally in preventing the guns from being worked.' He further stated that the report of Secretary Welles 'confirmed the worst estimate that we (the English) had formed of them.' The unprejudiced lecturer further told his hearers that the only Federal vessel that had ventured within 700 yards of Fort Sumter, the Keokuk, had to be withdrawn in a sinking condition, and afterward sunk. 'The eleven-inch guns proved too much for the eleven-inch turrets of the monitors,' added the lecturer, leaving his hearers to infer that the Keokuk was a monitor whose turret and hull had been riddled by Confederate balls. Our readers will bear in mind that this statement was made on the 18th of January, 1864, on an occasion of more than ordinary gravity, the subject under consideration being the great national question of harbor defence and the fortifications at Spithead. Captain Tyler produced charts showing that there were three distinct channels, varying from 1,000 to 3,000 yards in width, open to an enemy's vessels, and which channels he said could not be obstructed, yet, as the Keokuk had been sunk at a distance of 700 yards, these channels could not be entered by our iron-clads.

"We will not attempt to dispel Captain Tyler's delusion, nor question the soundness of his argument in proof of England's security. Our object is simply to point out that he has grossly misrepresented our naval achievements. The fact is, the Royal Engineers have been forced to admit the impregnability of our turrets and port-stoppers—hence their annoyance. The brevity of the action with the Confederate iron-clad Atlanta has shown that the 'cheese-box on a raft' is something more than a mere Yankee notion. The English artillerists are surprised to find that while they require twenty men to handle a ten-inch gun on land, our enormous pieces of fifteen-inch calibre are handled on board of the monitors with half a dozen hands—a single man only being required to point these guns. But more surprising still, the turrets and the port-stoppers offer absolute protection to guns, and gunners.

"The lecturer of the 18th of January knew that the monitors had been repeatedly engaged with the Confederate batteries at short ranges, since the first conflict at Charleston, and he well knew, at the time when he addressed his audience, that upwards of 2,000 shot had hit the monitor fleet. The Patapsco, it was well known at the time, had been in twenty-eight engagements, yet nothing had been destroyed within her turret, and not the slightest derangement caused to her machinery. These stubborn facts Captain Tyler cannot grapple with, and therefore tells his hearers what happened during the first brief trial of the new system, under fire at Charleston in April, 1863 A port-stopper which had been placed too near the turret in one of the vessels, stuck. The application of hammer and chisel for half an hour removed the difficulty. Not a single accident of the kind has occurred during the whole siege, not a pound of Confederate metal has entered through plates or port-stoppers ; and yet an officer in Her Majesty's service, before an audience composed of distinguished persons, ventures to state that ' the turrets of the monitors, and their port-stoppers, were effective principally in preventing the guns from being worked,' and that the Confederate guns ' proved too much for the eleven-inch plates which composed the turrets of the monitors.'

"We forbear comment, but advise the English people not to be lulled into security by assurances based on professional conceit and ignorance. Their neighbors over the Channel have fully proved that iron-clads, of the European type, are unfit to fight at sea, and that notwithstanding M. Xavier Raymond's splendid account of their success, written to order for *Revue des Deux Mondes*, just published, something better must be contrived. Accordingly, the Emperor of the French, through his agents, is taking a very careful look into our turrets. England will do well to do the same ; for with a single opponent at Cherbourg, such as our large turret vessels, with their fifteen-inch thick iron protection to their enormous guns, and ten and a half inch side-armor, backed by four feet of oak, the Warriors, Black Princes and Prince Consorts could not hold the channel for a single day. The experiments at the Washington Navy Yard established the fact long ago, that the four and a half inch plating of the European iron-clads with its thin wood backing, affords no protection against the enormous weight of ordnance which is part of the monitor system. The result of the recent trials of armor-plate instituted by the Navy Department, which we alluded to a few days ago, will amaze our Trans-Atlantic rivals. The news of the fate of the famous six-inch solid armor-plates, considered by the French as impregnable, will be most unwelcome. The utter demolition of Messrs. Petin and Gaudit's six-inch plate at the first shot from a fifteen-inch gun at Washington Navy Yard, on the 10th of February, 1864, will form an epoch in the history of iron-clads. The small-bore and high-velocity theory has received its quietus by this last practical mode adopted by the Navy Department for settling the question. Much credit is due to the Assistant Secretary of the Navy for his persistent course in adhering to the large smooth-bore principle, the successful application of which now enables us to defy all European iron-clads.

"It would appear that the great problem is nearer to solution than has been supposed. We have guns that can tear to fragments six-inch solid armor-plates at a single shot, and therefore fully adequate to crush in the sides of any European iron-clad. We operate these guns within impregnable iron cylinders 15 inches thick, which at the will of the gunner turn to any point of the compass. These cylinders again we place on vessels, which, while they present a very small target to the enemy's fire, are protected by ten-inch side-armor, backed by timber from three to four feet in thickness. In regard to speed, those who are best informed expect that our large turret ships will be very fast. We abstain from all speculation on this point, since the *Dictator* will be under steam by the end of April. It will be proper to add that our rivals have frequently asserted that our small monitor vessels would be useless for defensive purposes, notwithstanding their heavy and well-protected guns. They have boasted of their superior speed, and told us that their Warriors would run down the small Monitors, pass our forts and come up to our wharves.

"It has just occurred to them that their armored ships draw 25 feet water, while the monitors only draw 10½ feet, and that the gunner in a monitor turret, safe on the shoals along the main channels, can unmolested and at short range put his fifteen-inch shot through the insufficient armor of the intruder.

"We are informed that the Secretary of the Navy intends to send the *Dictator* on a trial-trip across the Atlantic next summer. We advise Capt. Tyler then to visit the American iron-clad, to learn if turrets and port-stoppers, as built in the United States, are 'effective principally in preventing the guns from being worked.'"

The Dunderberg is another monstrous iron-clad, much larger than either the Puritan or the Dictator, and very different in form, size, and general construction from any previously described. This is being built at the ship-yard of W. H. Webb, New York, and will soon be ready for launching. The following description will give a general idea of this powerful ship. It is copied from the SCIENTIFIC AMERICAN, of March 14, 1863 :

"The formidable ram-frigate Dunderberg, now building for the Government by W. H. Webb, at his yard at the foot of Sixth street, in this city, is in a very forward state, and being completed as fast as possible. We lately visited this vessel, and are able to furnish a few details of her construction, which we think will prove acceptable to our readers.

"The hull of the Dunderberg is massive, being solid from stem to stern. It is 378 feet long, 68 feet wide, and 32 feet deep. The frames are twelve inches thick, and are built of oak, firmly bolted and fastened together.

" The model of the ship is very peculiar. The floor is dead flat for the whole length, and the sides rise from it at an angle everywhere save forward, where they are very near vertical. The bow is as sharp and has as fine lines as it is possible to give it ; and the stern and run aft are very clean and handsomely modelled. The hull is divided by several water-tight compartments, both longitudinally and transversely—a precaution common to nearly all modern sea-going ships, which has been found indispensable. The frames are strapped diagonally with heavy irons, five inches wide by seven-eighths of an inch thick, blunt bolted to them. There is a slight sheer on deck, but it is almost invisible to the casual observer at a short distance. There is but one rudder : provision is made, however, for steering by an auxiliary apparatus of a peculiar nature, should the main steering-gear be shot away. The frame-timbers, twelve inches thick, are ceiled inside five inches thick, planked outside five inches thick, and over the planking two courses of heavy oak beams, twelve inches thick, are again laid, making in all an aggregate amount of nearly five feet of solid timber on the ram's sides. The planking is all caulked, and the seams payed, before the last protection is applied, and the entire mass is as firmly bolted together as it is possible to do it.

" The ram on the Dunderberg is about as formidable a looking object as one can conceive. The entire fore-foot of the vessel is prolonged thirty feet from the hull proper, and, rising easily upward from the keel about half the distance from the water-line, is there rounded, presenting a blunt end in shape like the profile of an axe-edge ; it then runs back toward the stem again. The mass of wood which forms this ram projects inside the hull almost as far as it does outboard, and is there substantially secured to the main timbers. The sides and edge of the ram will be iron-plated ; and even should the whole of it be knocked off in an affray, the builders say that the hull will be water-tight.

" The Dunderberg has, on top of the main-deck, casemated quarters for the guns and crew. This casemate slopes

at an acute angle from the sides to the top. It takes up a
large portion of the vessel amid-ships, and is an elongated
octagon in shape. It is made of heavy timber, plated with
iron four and a half inches thick. It is pierced on each side
for three broadside guns, and has one port forward and another aft, in the casemate, for bow and stern firing. The
hull of the ship is built out from a distance below the water-
line to meet the edge of the casemate above, so that the
broadside of the Dunderberg will present an acute angle to
the line of the enemy's fire. We do not know what the in-
clination of the casemate and side is, but it cannot be less
than 45°. The mass of wood and iron presenting a resistance
to the enemy's rams or projectiles at this point amounts in
all to seven feet. There are to be two turrets on the top of
this casemate. The thickness of the turret-walls will be
much greater than those of the Monitor batteries, and strong
enough to resist the heaviest ordnance.

" The armament of the Dunderberg has been variously
guessed at by parties. As it is not publicly known what it
will be, we are not able to inform our readers, further than
that rumor assigns the twenty-inch guns to the broadside,
while each turret will also contain two heavy guns. The
deck of the casemate, and also the main-deck, will be
plated bomb-proof; and the quarters for the officers and
crew, being in the fortress on deck, will be thoroughly ventilated and open to the light and air : there will then be none
of that depressing influence which is so marked in the depart-
ments assigned to the crews on the other batteries.

" One great and overwhelming advantage that this splendid vessel has, is that she is built of wood. She may leak,
become water-logged, roll, pitch, and toss, but there will still
be some hope for the crew as long as they stick to her. Iron
batteries fill and plunge out of sight with very little warning.
The effect of this fact upon sailors morally is not the least
important one. Although no men could have behaved better than the crew of the Monitor did in their peril, yet they
all felt that their case was hopeless ; and if they were saved,

it would be more the result of good fortune than any aid which their ship could afford them. The Dunderberg will draw about twenty feet of water. Her speed is not stated. Her engines are estimated at 6,000-horse-power. We are not able at present to give particulars of them."

This is one of the largest war-ships in the world, and quite different from all others yet devised.

If to these descriptions is added an account of some of the iron-clads intended for the rivers, the reader will have the means of forming a correct opinion of the mailed navy of the United States in its present condition. The gunboats Lafayette and Tuscumbia have been selected as types of our most powerful river iron-clads.

The Lafayette is 304 feet long, fifty feet beam, and draws eight and a half feet of water. Her plating is two and a half inches thick, backed by two inches of India rubber and twelve inches of solid oak. Her armament consists of two 200-pounder Parrott guns, two 100-pounder Parrott guns, and four nine-inch Dahlgrens.

The description of the Tuscumbia is taken from the SCIENTIFIC AMERICAN:

"The Tuscumbia is one among the largest vessels in the Western fleet. In strength of timbers, imperviousness of her coat of iron mail, stanchness of build, and completeness of outfit, she will rank among the very best of the iron-clads yet built. Her length is 182 feet, breadth of beam 70 feet, depth of hold 8 feet. She will draw five and a half feet of water, with all her armament, stores, coal, etc., aboard.

"Her machinery is of superior finish and extraordinary strength, and is all below the iron-clad deck, and is constructed upon an entirely new plan, lately approved and adopted by the Navy. She has two cylinders, thirty inches in diameter, six feet stroke, working two powerful side-wheels twenty-five feet in diameter, twelve feet bucket. She is also supplied with two other cylinders, twenty inches' stroke, working two screw propellers six feet six inches in diameter. She is furnished with two small engines for working the capstan, one forward and the other aft. She has six twenty-eight feet boilers forty inches in diameter, with five flues each, with an auxiliary pumping engine for filling the boilers. By her pumps the vessel could be flooded in a short time.

"The Tuscumbia has, in addition to her armament, an apparatus for throwing hot water, capable of ejecting a scalding stream to a distance of two hundred feet. The armament consists of three eleven-inch Dahlgren guns, in battery, forward, and two 100-pounder rifled guns, in battery, aft. The iron plating on the batteries or gun-rooms is six inches in thickness forward, and four inches thick aft. The sides of the vessel are plated with three-inch wrought iron ; the deck with one-inch wrought iron.

"The cost of the Tuscumbia will be about $250,000. Her magazines are provided with an apparatus by which they can be completely flooded in the short space of one minute. A bulwark of iron, loop-holed, for musketry, is placed around her guards. Her speed will be about twelve miles an hour against the current. She will be manned by 150 marines. Her custom-house measurement is 980 tons."

It must not, however, be thought that these two boats represent nearly all the Western iron-clads. They are of many different forms, and vary greatly in their armament and general efficiency. Many of them are expensive and powerful vessels. Some of those lately constructed have turrets ; and the form of these has been varied, in order to try experiments which might settle important questions of construction. Their armament, in general, is very heavy— nearly all of them carrying one or more guns of greater calibre than can be found on the largest French and English frigates. Eleven-inch smooth-bores and 200-pounder rifles are common guns on board the larger class of the river iron-clad gunboats. They have been used successfully against fortifications armed with the largest cannon, rifled and smooth-bore, which the rebels have, and have proved a most efficient arm of the nation's power.

The only broadside ocean-ships which the Americans have yet plated with iron, except the Roanoke, which has an exposed side and turrets also, are the small corvette Galena and the New Ironsides frigate. It is stated that the Galena was mailed with plates three and a half inches thick. She was pierced and nearly ruined by ten-inch shot in the fight at Fort Darling, while the same kind of shot made no serious impression on the armor of the Monitor.

The New Ironsides is a first-class frigate, whose tonnage, according to the register, is about 3,500 tons. She is, therefore, somewhat larger than the Minnesota, and about 1,000 tons less in burden than the Niagara. Her armor-plates are four and a half inches thick; and her armament consists of fourteen eleven-inch smooth-bores, two 150-pounder rifles, two 50-pounder rifles, and two howitzers.

Her broadside, therefore, is very nearly the same with that of the Warrior in weight; but her principal shot weigh 170 and 150 pounds, while those of the English frigate weigh 68 and 100 pounds—the latter used in Armstrong guns.

Such guns as the New Ironsides carries defeated the Merrimac, though the Monitor had only two of them; while the Ironsides has been exposed at Charleston to far more formidable guns than any yet used on an English, or, indeed, on any European ship, and has received in all those battles no serious injury. The Charleston correspondent of the London TIMES describes her broadside as the most terrible one in its effects ever thrown from a ship. Except in speed, this ship has fully answered the expectation of the country. She was constructed, however, with a more anxious care to obtain a powerful and invulnerable battery than to give her unusual speed. The broadside ship and the Monitor batteries are designed for different spheres of action; and while swiftness is desirable in both, it seems more important for the broadside ship that is intended for an ocean cruiser.

It must be remembered, when comparing the armament of American and European ships, that changes are continually going on ; and the indications are that England is disposed to follow our lead in the adoption of heavy guns ; and we may expect to see some of her new ships armed with the largest guns which she is able to fabricate. It is announced, for instance, that the Royal Sovereign, a turreted ship, is to carry 300-pounder guns. As yet, England has not produced a reliable cannon of this size, much less has she mounted one on the deck of a ship. But if Americans teach her the art, she will do it hereafter. Our largest wooden frigates, such as the Wabash, the Minnesota, and the Niagara, are ships of only medium speed, but they are heavily armed with the most formidable cannon which have ever been used, except those on board the Monitors. As an example, the Niagara, which has been undergoing extensive repairs, in the hope of increasing her speed, lately took on board, as her armament, twenty-four eleven-inch smooth-bore guns and twelve 200-pounder Parrott rifles, with which the weight of her broadside would be 3,200 pounds—twice that, or nearly so, of the English Warrior. This armament, however, was found to sink the ship too low in the water, and it has been changed. The case, however, indicates the direction of American experiments. Our new corvettes, such as the Lackawanna and the Canandaigua, are very swift ships, and, in size, are nearly equal to the old form of the line-of-battle ship, while their armament is far more formidable.

This general survey of the American navy may be completed by stating, that among our smaller vessels are some of the swiftest in the world.

AMERICAN ARTILLERY.

It will be seen, from the foregoing statements, that the comparative efficiency of the new American navy depends upon two things : the American, or Ericsson form of the turreted ship, and the power of our new artillery. If the Monitor batteries are really invulnerable, yet, if they are not armed with guns that can shatter or pierce the sides of an enemy's ship, they would be nearly worthless; while the superiority and even the safety of our ships of other forms must depend upon the character of their guns.

Other nations as well as our own are earnestly engaged in costly experiments with artillery. What they may hereafter produce, of course, none now can know; but, up almost to the present hour, the effort of the artillerists of Europe has been to obtain the highest possible velocity for the shot, the greatest possible power of penetration, sacrificing to these ends the weight of the projectile.

The American theory, on the contrary, has been to increase the weight of the shot, at the expense of its velocity if necessary—to use, in any event, for breaching walls and smashing armor-plates, a heavy projectile, and then, by rifling or otherwise improving the gun, to increase velocity and range.

Acting upon these opposite theories, the English have mounted, as yet, upon their ships no smooth-bore cannon larger than the eight-inch 68-pounder, which forms the principal broadside guns of the Warrior; while the Americans have already in actual service, on their vessels, nine-inch, ten-inch, eleven-inch, and fifteen-inch smooth-bore guns, while a twenty-inch gun has just been cast at Pittsburg, said to be intended for the Dunderberg; and 200-pounder rifles are found on even our gunboats, and 300-pounder Parrott rifles are in our batteries at Charleston.

Before stating facts in regard to American cannon which might seem an empty boast, it may be well to present some very late English opinions upon our new artillery. The first extract is from the Richmond correspondent of the London TIMES, and, of course, not inclined to over-estimate an American invention:

" Again I feel tempted to raise a warning voice about the disparity of the armament on board of the English and American navies. It is impossible for those who have been many months absent from England to be well informed as to the actual state of public opinion at the present moment upon this vital subject. But, judging from the officers of Her Majesty's navy who have, at rare intervals, brought vessels of war into Confederate ports, it appears still to be held that the 68-pounder or eight-inch smooth-bore is England's best weapon of offence against iron-clad vessels. The experience gained at Charleston enables me confidently to affirm, that as well might you pelt one of the Yankee Monitors or the Ironsides with peas as expect them to be in any way damaged by eight-inch shot.

"Another disagreeable question forces itself upon an Englishman's attention when he is cognizant of the terrific broadside thrown by the eight eleven-inch guns of the Ironsides—one of the most formidable broadsides, in the opinion of the defenders of Charleston, which has ever been thrown by any vessel upon earth. Have we any ship in existence which could successfully resist such a broadside, and respond to it with anything like commensurate weight and vigor? I should be faithless to my duty if I did not mention that it is the universal opinion of all the English officers serving in the Confederate army, with whom I conversed, that England is behind America in the weight and power of the guns sent by both nations to sea.

"It is still a matter of the greatest surprise to those who are cognizant of the endless experiments in guns and projectiles which are every day made by the Federal and Confederate States, that England has not thought it worth her while to attach to the armies of both nations such a commission as McClellan had in the Crimean war, with a view to their gaining such scientific information with regard to ordnance and projectiles as at this moment can be gained nowhere else on earth. It is my conviction that from both sections such commissioners would receive nothing but courteous and unreserved information upon all that it imported them to know. It is scarcely creditable to our Government that they should be blind to the opportunities for gaining information which this gigantic conflict affords, or that, from Old World pride, they should refuse to avail themselves of the experience to be derived from a continent destined henceforth and evermore to play no secondary part in the drama of the world."

The second opinion is taken from the ARMY AND NAVY GAZETTE (London):

"It may be concluded as certain that the guns used by Gillmore were Parrott's rifled ordnance. Their work has been effectually done. Had such guns been available in the trenches before Sebastopol, the Allies would have made short work, not only of the Redan and Malakoff, and *bastion du mât*, but of the shipping and of the forts at the other side of the harbor. It must not be supposed that Sumter was a flimsy, gingerbread fort. It was constructed of a peculiar kind of hard, close brick, six and seven feet thick; the arches of the casemates and the supporting pillars were of eight and nine feet thickness. The faces presented to the breaching batteries must have subtended, at 3,500 yards, an exceedingly small angle, and the elevation of the fort was low. But so great was the accuracy of the fire, that a vast proportion of the shots struck it; so great the penetration, that the brickwork was perforated 'like a rotten cheese;' so low the trajectory, that the shot, instead of plunging into, passed through the fort, and made clean breaches through both walls. Now, the guns that did this work cost, we believe, just one-fourth of our ordnance, cwt. for cwt.; they are light and very easily handled. The gun itself is finely rifled, with grooves varying from four and five in number, for small calibres, to six and seven for the larger; but, as Mr. Parrott is still 'experimenting,' no settled plan has been arrived at, and all we know is that the pitch is not so sharp as is the case in our rifled guns. The projectile is like the conical Armstrong, and has a leaden sabot and coating—at least it is coated and based with some soft metal.

"In this journal the attention of the Government authorities has been called, again and again, to the Parrott and Dahlgren guns. The Americans have constructed cannon of calibres which to us are known only as of theoretical and probable attainment, and they have armed batteries hundreds of miles from their arsenals, with the most powerful guns ever used in war, which have been carried by sea and in stormy waters to the enemy's shores. Before such projectiles as these guns carry, the breaching of masonry, whether of brick or stone, is a question of short time. And, in face of these facts, we are obliged to record that our scientific officers are of opinion that our 'best gun for breaching purposes is the old 68-pounder!' Why, we know what that can do! We know that at 3,500 yards its fire would be about as effectual as that of Mons. Meg. These trials at two hundred yards are perfectly fatuous, if no other results than these, or such as these, be gained by them. It is of no use saying Sumter was of brick; it was at least as good a work as most of our existing fortifications, and infinitely less easy 'to splinter up' than a work of granite or rubble masonry. In substance it resembled very much our martello towers on the beach at Hythe. Have we any gun which could breach one of these at 3,500 yards? . . . The authorities have had no experience of the effect of such shot as the Dahlgrens propel. They have not got the guns to discharge them. When next the ordnance officers and gentlemen meet, let them apply their minds to the little experiments the Americans have been making for their benefit at Sumter. It is astounding to see what progress has been made in artillery since the Crimean war."

Another English periodical, by no means favorable to Americans, makes the following observations upon the operations at Charleston:

"'The Swamp Angel,' as the Federals call the big gun of General Gillmore, has surely bellowed loud enough at Sumter to wake up some of our critics at home *to what is a fact in despite of them.* As they have underestimated the civil contest, so they have overlooked the Titanic character of the military duel, peddling and muddling over strategies on the map, and blind, meanwhile, to the revolution which these giant combatants are accomplishing in the art of warfare. If the Americans are vain of being 'big,' why not do them the justice of confessing that they attain that adjec-

tive, in their contentions, their sufferings, and their engines
and methods of warfare? Twice in the course of this two-
years' struggle they have altered the complexion of the science of destruction—once on the water, and once on land.
The Monitor and Merrimac confessedly initiated a new era
in naval tactics. The plates of both are hardly rusted by
the salt-water into which they went down so soon; but
already every country that pretends to keep the sea armed is
fitting out vessels after their kind. Now, it is a revolution
in the art of attack by battery and defense by battlements,
which these energetic fighters have developed. Sumter is
down—breached and shattered into such a ruin that hardly
one stone stands upon another. And this, after repeated
failure with such artillery as could be made to float aboard
ship, has been accomplished by enormous cannon fixed on a
land-battery, discharging bolts of two hundred pounds'
weight, at a range of four thousand four hundred yards.
Six hundred of these Olympian thunderbolts were hurled
across this interval upon the walls and parapets of Sumter
during the course of three days, and with such deadly accuracy that the proud keystone fortress of Charleston Harbor
withered under them; and an eyewitness writes, that a
moldy cheese fired at for a month with pistols could not
present a more forlorn appearance than Fort Sumter at the
close of the bombardment. No arsenal is safe, no empire
secure, which is too proud to study this lesson. Neverthe-
less, what is chiefly remarkable about the destruction of
Sumter is the range at which it was accomplished, and the
precision of the fire by which these huge bolts were flung.
The 200-pounders are said to have gone through and
through, till the further channel of the fort could be seen
between the gaping rents and fissures of the double wall.
Neither Mr. Whitworth nor Sir William Armstrong has
shown us anything in range and accuracy like this. The
American officers have, first in their profession, laid, and
kept at work throughout three days, siege-guns the like of
which for weight were last used when Mohammed besieged
Constantinople. We do not hesitate to say that our Spit-

head forts must be reconsidered, as to structure and position, if our enemies, whoever they may be, can be made to fire these American guns from their floating batteries."

The facts upon which these Englishmen have been compelled to review and change their opinions of American affairs are such as all Americans should know and study, and they are presented to the reader, in order that he may feel confidence in American genius, and know the nature and power of our new weapons of war. It is proposed to confine these statements to our largest cannon, for they alone are peculiarly American. The 300-pounder Parrott gun is the most destructive one, at long ranges, which has as yet been used, either in this country or elsewhere.

Its range is between five and six miles, and Charleston has been effectually shelled at a distance of five miles. This gun, as is said, has thrown its shot through nine inches of solid iron.

The 200-pounder Parrott rifle has a range scarcely less than the former; and with these guns Sumter was riddled and demolished at the distance of two miles and a half—a feat before unheard of in all the records of war. In the destruction of Fort Sumter the Monitors and the New Ironsides assisted, but the work was performed mainly by the land-batteries, because the destruction was certain without exposure of the fleet, and with little loss of life. Some of the Monitors are armed with one of these guns, and one fifteen-inch one. The shot of the fifteen-inch gun weighs 425 pounds, and the shell 334 pounds. These monster guns, being as yet experiments, have been handled very cautiously in regard to the charges of powder. In the trial of this gun at Fortress Monroe, General Barnard, of the Engineer Corps, says the shell, with a charge of forty pounds of large-grained powder, had an initial velocity of 1,328 feet per second, and a range of more than three miles, with 28° 35' elevation.

He gives his opinion that the maximum range of this gun is " considerably beyond four miles." It has been lately found that these, as well as our other large cast-iron smooth-bores, will bear charges heavier than those hitherto used. The French armor-plates are said to be superior in resisting power to the English ones. A French plate, six inches thick, and prepared especially for a target, was lately, at the Washington Navy Yard, smashed in pieces by a single shot from one of these fifteen-inch guns.

"While rifle seacoast guns give vastly increased accuracy, range, and penetration at the higher elevations, the effect upon armored vessels of their projectiles of relatively smaller diameter is very much less destructive than the smashing shock of the immense iron spheres projected from the thirteen, the fifteen, or the twenty-inch.

"There is no longer any question of the fact, that the introduction of guns which project such enormous spheres of iron have restored to forts their pristine superiority over ships. No *sea-going* armored vessel can withstand the shock of a fifteen-inch shot; and it is believed that a thirteen-inch, or even a ten-inch solid shot, will be found to be quite as effective. It is, therefore, safe to assert, that our harbors, defended by forts armed with such guns, and having the advantage of artificial submarine obstructions, are securely barred against any ship that can cross the ocean. The wreck produced by the impact of these mighty spheres will set at defiance the most energetic efforts of ships' pumps or ship-carpenters' plugs; and, as in the case of the brief but eloquent duel of the Weehawken and the Atlanta, the men of which latter vessel were driven below from their guns, and could not be induced to return to them, it produces a moral effect as irresistible as it is fatal."

The armor of the Atlanta, equal, as is said, to five inches of solid iron, was pierced by a shot from a fifteen-inch gun, and the ship captured.

The Government has lately constructed a thirteen-inch gun of the same external dimensions, or nearly so, as the fifteen-inch gun. It is supposed that this will bear a much heavier charge of powder, and the velocity and range of the shot be proportionately greater. To test the penetrating and smashing power of cannon-shot, a ten-inch gun was lately loaded heavily and fired at an iron target ten inches thick, and the ball pierced it through.

The heavy Parrott rifles will pierce armor-plates of four inches' and five inches' thickness with ease. The 300-pounder smashes a nine-inch plate; and Stafford's projectiles, thrown from a cast-iron smooth-bore, have gone through seven inches of solid iron, with only fourteen pounds of powder.

These facts, in connection with what has been before stated, will enable one to judge of the comparative power of our navy, and our means of attack and defence. The reader must remember that the results already reached are the first fruits only of American genius when earnestly applied to the arts of war; and that experiments are even now going on which promise still more formidable cannon than any now in use.

In estimating the power of our weapons, the reader must not forget that the old solid cast-iron spherical shot and the spherical shell are no longer the most formidable projectiles used in cannon. Elongated shot and shells of many different forms are used in our rifled cannon, and lately such projectiles have been used in our smooth-bores, and even in the fifteen-inch guns. According to Captain Rodgers' report, it was, however, a spherical shot from a fifteen-inch gun which smashed the side of the Atlanta, and drove the crew in a panic from their guns—the eleven-inch gun having failed to injure her.

Some of these elongated missiles, whose length is about twice and a half their diameter, are rounded like a cone, some are flat-headed, some have the end formed like a punch, some are cast iron, some are of chilled iron, some have case-hardened ends, some are of wrought iron, and some are of steel. These last are said to be the most destructive shot which have yet been tried, so far as penetration is concerned; but whether these or the smashing heavy shot—a 425-pounder—would soonest destroy a ship or fort, is a question yet to be tried.

The reader can now form an intelligent opinion of the

comparative power for attack and resistance of the American
and the European iron-clad. But before the direct comparison is made, let the following statement be carefully read.
It is the opinion of one of the most competent judges of
such matters in this country—the editor of the SCIENTIFIC
AMERICAN—upon the condition of the Monitors after the
attack upon Sumter; an opinion formed, as is shown, after a
personal inspection of the vessel most injured in the fight :

" Now that the smoke of battle has cleared away, and
the fearful cannonading at Fort Sumter, which so annoyed
the twittering reporters, has ceased, we may review the event
dispassionately and with reason, at least in so far as it con-
cerns the offensive and defensive powers of the Monitors.
The daily press, through its accredited representatives, made
great haste to assure the public that their favorite batteries,
those in which (not unwisely) they placed the greatest confidence, were altogether unsuitable, and, in fact, were not
available against heavy artillery. At the time we were compelled, against our judgment, in view of the overwhelming
representations of these self-constituted authorities, to accept
as a fact that we were beaten in the contest, and compelled
to retire from the fort by sheer force alone. Even at the
time of the action, and in days supervening, that portion of
the press of the country who criticised the conduct of the
attack were immediately frowned down, and, to say the
least, sent to ' Coventry ' by other papers, whose interests or
opinions led them to sustain the part our commanders took
on that occasion. We were treated with graphic accounts
of the effects of the rebel shot on the Monitor's turrets ; and
it was asserted that the most destructive shot that was fired
on the occasion struck the Passaic's turret near the top, and,
after scooping out an immense portion of it, broke all the
eleven plates, and spent its force on the pilot-house, which it
very nearly demolished. This is the spirit, if not the exact
letter, of the accounts furnished. Now, we have examined
the turret of the Passaic since her arrival here for repairs,
and, with all due respect for the *reporter's* rhetoric and his

sensational paragraph, we must say that it is *bosh*. The shot *did* strike the turret, *did* scoop out a portion (which might weigh twenty-five pounds), and *did* strike the pilot-house with great force, besides breaking the turret-plates in its passage. But what of all this? When iron meets iron (as when Greek meets Greek), then comes the tug of war; and it is not to be supposed that a shot, moving at the rate of say 1,500 feet per second, will strike an iron structure in its weakest part and not damage it.

"The simple facts of this loudly-trumpeted performance of the rebels are, that the shot which struck the Passaic did not endanger her safety in the least; for all the effect they had on her externally, she might have been fighting away till this hour, and, in reality, have been none the worse for it. We have examined the shot-marks on the Passaic, said to be sixty-eight in all, though we did not count them, and find an accurate representation of the Whitworth shot impressed in the turret in many places. If these much-boasted projectiles are not able to do any greater damage than they did, we may safely defy all the English iron-clads and their armaments. The Whitworth shot, or *fac similes* of them, in a majority of cases, struck sideways; they reached the turret in all possible positions, and show very poor shooting on the part of the rebels. There were several bolts driven in on the turret, which injured the persons within; but the majority of the indentations and scars could be covered by and filled with a common tea-saucer. These are, simply, the 'terrible' effects of the rebel shot. Now, what person possessing ordinary judgment, and at all conversant with the properties of iron, could conscientiously report that the Monitors were unable to cope with artillery? For our own part, we assert that the favorable opinions hitherto expressed in regard to those vessels have been greatly strengthened, and we do not hesitate to say, that, with the present artillery, they can successfully defy any fort or any iron-clad afloat. So far as the impregnability of their armor is involved, we would not hesitate an instant to confide our personal safety to the thickness of their walls. We have no

desire to disparage any official in connection with this subject; but, so far as the Monitors being disabled (except tem-
porarily) in the late attack is concerned, we must avow our
utter skepticism. The Passaic is the only iron-clad sent
North; *ergo*, the Passaic must be the one most injured.
What injuries are those that merely indent iron plates! and
what terrible shot those must be which strike and leave no
sign internally to tell the story of their spent force and im-
potent rage! We think a much better sensational report
could have been made on the occasion by writing the facts:
How the minions of the rebel Government did their utmost
to demolish the Monitors, and how signally they failed;
how, backed and aided by English capital and skill, they
hurled their powerful projectiles against the impenetrable
iron-clads, and were worsted in the encounter; how grandly
those little vessels withstood the enemy's fury; and how,
saving one poor little egg-shell craft, they bore unflinchingly
the most furious cannonading that was ever known in the
shortest space of time. These features would have been
worth commenting upon; and were we in the rebels' situa-
tion, we should prefer a naval assault to take any shape but
that proceeding from a fleet of those vessels. Properly
handled and armed, they can defy any ship now floating;
and improvements are being made which will render their
utility past all doubt.

"We have considered in this light merely the question
of the impregnability of the Monitors—supposed to be the
first requisite of a modern war-vessel. That they have other
objectionable features, we do not deny; but, taking them as
representatives of fighting machines—the greatest offensive
power in the very smallest compass—they cannot be excelled,
and the nation does well to estimate them among its stanchest
defences.

"It is singular, in viewing the effects of the shot on the
Passaic's turret, to note that they exhibit none of the characteristics of a plunging fire. The shot that 'scooped out a
tremendous portion' of the top of the Passaic's turret, struck
the pilot-house at nearly the same height, showing that it

must have been fired at point-blank range, or nearly so. So also those that struck the base of the turret—no marks are visible on the deck which would lead the observer to suppose that the missiles were fired from such an elevation as the barbette of Fort Sumter; and we conjecture that the batteries on Morris Island and Battery Bee must have taken a hand in the engagement, although we think it is stated in the reports that those batteries were silent."

Let it be remembered that every form of missile, shot, and shell which English skill and capital could supply, was hurled at the Monitors in that fight, and at short range, and then, in the light of the foregoing statement, judge of their powers of endurance. Let it now be supposed that one of these our smallest Monitors were to engage such a ship as the English Warrior, and let us observe the combatants. Let them be placed so that each is within range of the other's guns. The Monitor carries two guns; the Warrior has forty. Of the Monitor's guns, one is a fifteen-inch smooth-bore, the other a 200-pounder Parrott rifle. The Warrior has twenty-eight 68-pounder smooth-bores and twelve 100-pounder Armstrong rifles. First observe the difference in the surface which each presents to the other's fire when lying broadside opposed to broadside. This would not often be the case in action, perhaps, but it is the only method of making a comparison. The exact height of the Warrior above the water is not known to the writer. The battery of the Gloire is said to be six feet above the water, and the lower battery of the Normandie is eight feet, and these are said to be lower than in the English frigates, and too low for service in a rough sea.

Without pretending to entire accuracy—nor is this necessary—it will probably be safe to estimate the sides of the Warrior as rising eighteen feet above the water, from the water-line to the top of her bulwarks. She is about three hundred and eighty feet long, and her broadside presents, therefore, in round numbers, 6,800 square feet to an enemy's fire. The small Monitors, such as those at Charleston, are two hundred feet long. Their decks are, at most, it is said, not more than twelve inches above the water, and this narrow strip of hull and the turret are all that is exposed. The turret is about twenty-two feet outside diameter, by nine feet high, presenting a surface of not quite two hundred feet. The hull and the turret together, then, offer a surface of about four hundred square feet to fire, compared with the more than 6,000 square feet of the Warrior's broadside.

Here, then, is at once an immense advantage in favor of the Monitor. Her chances of being struck, at the distance of a mile, would be exceedingly small, while at that distance the huge hull of the broadside frigate would be almost certainly hit by a majority of shots fired. It is doubtless true that the ships in action would not often thus be exposed broadside to broadside; and yet it would seem that this might be the Warrior's safest position, for her bow and stern are unprotected with armor, and are as vulnerable as any wooden ship.

Let their comparative vulnerability be now considered. Experiment has conclusively shown that no gun now on board the Warrior, or any other European ship, can pierce the turret of a Monitor, or even materially injure her side. The bombardment from the Charleston forts has proved this beyond all contradiction. A Monitor, therefore, could not be materially injured by the Warrior's guns. On the other hand, the 200-pounder Parrott gun pierces armor like that of the Warrior with ease; the shot from the fifteen-inch gun pierced the Atlanta's armor, and a fifteen-inch gun has smashed plates much thicker than the armor of the English ship; and we have the opinion of General Barnard, already quoted, that no *sea-going*, armored ship can withstand the shock of a fifteen-inch shot.

All these facts go to show that the boasted Warrior would be overmatched by one of our small Monitors, like those at Charleston. This would inevitably be the case if she were restricted to the use of her guns only. But it is said that such a frigate could easily run down and sink a Monitor. It should be remembered that the huge frigate, almost four hundred feet long, is unwieldy, while the Monitors, only half as long, are easily manœuvred. It requires, as is said, fifteen minutes to turn the Warrior, and it may be seen, therefore, that it is probably a very difficult instead of an easy thing for a long, heavy frigate to run down a Monitor. The attacking ship would be much more likely to miss her foe, and receive the fifteen-inch and 200-pounder rifled shot at short range. It is true, a slow Monitor cannot pursue and capture a swift frigate like the Warrior; but when a pet ship of the English navy shall avoid a combat with a diminutive craft like a Monitor, it will do more to establish our supremacy on the sea, than to capture that frigate in battle. Should a European iron-clad ever visit our shores on a hostile errand, it will not endeavor to save itself from a Monitor by flight. In such a case the issue of battle must be tried.

But the Warrior is, probably, not now the most formidable ship in the English navy. As none of those iron-clads have been yet tested in battle, it is impossible to judge correctly their comparative merits. There are some new frigates, however, of about the Warrior's size, whose armor over the battery is stated to be, for one five inches, for another five and a half inches, and for still another six inches in thickness; and these ships are reported to have a speed of about twelve knots per hour. This was on the trial-trip, and, as with our own vessels, it will be much less in actual service.

Let it now be supposed that the most formidable one of this class, with an armor six inches thick in the central portion of the ship, the vessel being of the Warrior's size, were matched against one of our new Monitors, like the Agamenticus, the Monadnock, or the Miantonomoh.

These Monitors have a side-armor, as is stated, of ten and a half inches in thickness, while the turrets are fifteen inches thick. No shot yet fired, either here or in England, has penetrated such an armor as this; and such an armor cannot be placed upon a broadside ship of the common form: it would sink her at the dock. Between the English frigate Minotaur, part of whose armor is said to be six inches thick, and such a Monitor as the Agamenticus, there would be the same disparity before mentioned, in the surfaces exposed to shot. The Minotaur is more than four times the tonnage of such a Monitor, and while the deck of the Monitor lies almost level with the water, the Minotaur presents her huge broadside high above the water-line, and four hundred feet long. The Monitor, besides having this immense advantage in the chances of being hit by shot, is herself invulnerable to any cannon now in use; while the fifteen-inch gun she carries smashes through a six-inch plate of the best French manufacture, and her Parrott shot goes through plates six inches and even nine inches thick. How, then, will the Minotaur withstand the Monitor's attack? Nothing is plainer than that she cannot do it with her guns. Can the frigate run the Monitor down? It is useless to speculate upon the issue of such an experiment. The Monitors are also rams of a very formidable kind, and the broadside frigate, considering the effect of the Monitor's guns at short range, would, to say the least, be in as great peril as the American vessel. But if the Minotaur cannot run down such a Monitor, and should choose to continue the combat, it is a matter of certainty that she would be captured or sunk. But again: suppose any European ship of which we have any account should engage the Dictator. Her side-armor, more than eleven inches thick, and her turret, fifteen inches, cannot be pierced by any shot now known.

She, too, lies almost level with the water, presenting a small mark to her adversary, and, with half the tonnage of the Minotaur, she has engines of 5,000 indicated horse-power, while the Warrior and Minotaur have scarcely the same amount of engine-power. The Dictator, then, ought to be much the fastest vessel, but this must be determined by trial. Certainly, however, she cannot, with such engines, be a slow ship. She is built especially for a ram, and she will carry two guns of no less power than the fifteen-inch gun and the 300-pounder Parrott, because we know that we have those at command. But Mr. Ericsson is making his own guns for this new ship, to be applied hereafter, and

5

expects them to be more formidable than any now in use. Should he not succeed in this, we already have cannon in her turret, that, in the opinion of our best engineer officers, no sea-going ship can withstand. What chance would the Minotaur have with the Dictator?

Or, finally, select the most powerful broadside ship in the English navy, and place her by the side of Mr. Webb's immense frigate and ram combined, the Dunderberg. Her size is equal to the Minotaur, or nearly so. Her turrets cannot be penetrated; her casemates and sides are as well protected as those of the English ships; she will have engines of far greater power; and her guns will crash through any armor that a broadside ship can float. The reader can judge what the result of an engagement would be between any European ship now known, and either the Dictator, the Puritan, or the Dunderberg.

Compared with their tonnage and displacement, these ships have, by far, the most powerful engines ever placed on a war-ship. They ought to be the swiftest armed vessels afloat. This remains to be tried. Should they prove so, however, it is easy to see that England and France will once more be compelled to begin their navies anew, if they intend to attack the United States.

Such is the navy which the United States Government has created in a little more than two years; and, gigantic and efficient as it already is, it is but the first step in our new career—only the earnest, the first fruits, of what the nation is capable of performing. American genius has not yet reached the limit of its inventive power, and we have no reason to fear that it will not hereafter, as it has hitherto done, keep pace with the progress of Europe.

Mr. Ericsson's invention not only saved the country in an hour of great peril, but it will revolutionize the structure of war-ships, for the Monitors and the big guns, smooth-bore and rifled, have rendered it certain that no broadside ship can cross the ocean which our vessels cannot sink; and Mr. Webb's monster sea-going ram seems likely to present another American idea, which will attract the attention of the world.

The Government has been severely criticised for constructing so many Monitors, and no broadside and swift vessels. Events will probably vindicate the wisdom of those who have controlled the navy. The country needed, first of all, not so much swift ships, nor large ocean cruisers, to match the European navies, as batteries, for coast service, as nearly invulnerable as human skill and science *then* could make them.

This want was undeniably met by the Monitors better than it could have been by any other vessels yet known. It needed, at the same time, gunboats for the rivers. It will be conceded that these have done admirable service, and, so far as yet appears, the best of them will be used as models for future fleets. The broadside type of iron-clads was followed in the New Ironsides, and, notwithstanding she is one of the finest frigates of this class afloat, yet, as the improvements in cannon show how easily her armor can be pierced, no one will regret that these experiments in artillery have been made before we had expended $250,000,000, as England has done, in constructing broadside ships. If a fleet of iron-clad broadside ships is needed at any time hereafter, we can construct it with all the added light derived from the experiments of the world.

The country needed swift wooden cruisers for the work of the blockade, and the Navy Department has furnished from its own yards some of the fastest ships that float—vessels that overhaul the swiftest blockade runners that ever left an English port; and these ships are the beginning of a new class of American ships which, in speed and power of armament, are not yet matched elsewhere. Having produced such a navy in a little more than three years, and which is only the germ of the future American navy, with a commercial marine already greater than that even of England, with unlimited resources at command, with two great oceans washing a coast-line of thousands of miles, nothing seems too great to anticipate in regard to the future naval power of America.

We want, however, no fleets for conquest; we have no

wish to interfere with the affairs of other nations—as England and France have threatened, and still desire, in regard to us—and enough is already known to show them that, until some new war-ship shall be invented in Europe, no fleet can be sent to invade us that cannot be destroyed with the means we already have; and we may feel entire confidence that the genius of our inventors and the skill of our workmen will hereafter devise ships and guns that will protect, on every sea, the Stripes and Stars, which will represent, hereafter, a Free and Christian American Nation.

Letters have been addressed to the Secretary of the Navy, upon the subject of the Monitors and the fifteen-inch guns, by three of our most distinguished naval officers—Commodore Rodgers, Admiral Porter, and Admiral Dahlgren—whose opinions are so important that extracts from them are added here, for the views of such men in high official stations should be considered as decisive upon subjects with which they are perfectly familiar. Every American will feel encouraged, in regard to the present and future of the American navy, by these letters, while they cannot fail to make a profound impression on Europe.

In describing the difference between the ordinary ship and the Monitor model, Commodore Rodgers says:

"In the Ironsides class, the hull of a wooden man-of-war, as constructed for general purposes, is clad with iron. It is true, some modification of shape and increase of size is required to meet the additional weight which she has to carry; but still, in essentials, she is a vessel of the ordinary model; she has the advantage of ample quarters for her crew, with free access to her decks in storms; with natural ventilation; with abundance of light; with numerous guns, giving her a rapidity of fire unattainable in a Monitor, and essential in battering forts; and she is as able to carry canvas as other men-of-war.

"The Monitor class, as far as I know, is new. If I understand the idea, it is to cut off all the surface above water, except that which may be necessary to flotation, and to carry the guns in a revolving turret, or turrets, near the centre of motion, supported upon the keel and kelsons.

"The plans upon which Mr. Ericsson has worked out this idea of his may be modified by further experience; but the idea itself will be employed while iron-clad vessels are used in warfare."

He describes the advantage of the Ericsson model as follows:

"It has these advantages:
"The Monitor has the least possible surface to be plated, and therefore takes the least possible tonnage to float armor of a given thickness, or, with a given tonnage, allows the greatest possible thickness of armor, and, consequently, the greatest possible impregnability. The ability to carry armor is proportionable to the tonnage, but the Monitor of 844 tons has actually thicker plating than the Ironsides of 3,480 tons, and than the Warrior of 6,000; and yet the Ironsides and Warrior have only the middle portion of their hulls plated, their ends being merely of wood without armor.

"The guns of the Monitors, near the centre of motion, are supported upon the keel and kelsons, upborne by the depth of water under them, and carried by the whole strength of the hull.

"In Monitors heavier guns are, therefore, practicable than can ever be carried in broadside out upon the ribs of a ship.

"In the Monitors, concentration of guns and armor is the object sought.

"In them the plating is compressed into inches of elevation; while in the Ironsides class it is extended over feet; and the comparatively numerous guns distributed over the decks of the Ironsides class are moulded into a few larger ones in the turrets of the Monitors."

In speaking of the principle upon which the Monitors are armed, he says:

" When power enough is required in the individual guns to crush and pierce the side of an adversary at a single blow, the most formidable artillery must be employed—and fifteen-inch guns are the most formidable which, so far, we have tried ; but no vessel of the Ironsides class can carry these guns, and the Monitors actually do carry them. If target experiments are reliable, a shot from a fifteen-inch gun will crush in the side of any vessel of the Ironsides class in Europe or America. A single well-planted blow would sink either the Warrior, La Gloire, Magenta, Minotaur, or the Bellerophon."

Commodore Rodgers says, also, that the Monitors roll very little in a seaway, and relates the following incident to show their steadiness. A bottle of claret, he says, remained standing for an hour on the dinner-table of the Weehawken at a time when no one could stand on the deck of her convoy, the Iroquois, a fine sea-boat, without holding on to the life-lines.

Admiral Dahlgren declares that, to meet the wants of the Government in this war, the Monitors are far better than the broadside models adopted by France and England; and that, if contractors had met the Government demand, every Southern port would, ere this, have been in our possession.

Admiral Porter says that, with one of our Monitors, he could begin at Cairo, and, going down the Mississippi, destroy every vessel we have on the Western waters, unless they should escape by flight.

Commodore Rodgers states his conclusions as follows :

" To sum up my conclusions, I think that the Monitor class and the Ironsides class are different weapons, each having its peculiar advantages—both needed to an iron-clad navy—both needed in war ; but that, when the Monitor class measures its strength against the Ironsides class, then, with vessels of equal size, the Monitor class will overpower the Ironsides class ; and, indeed, a single Monitor will capture many casemated vessels of no greater individual size or speed : and as vessels find their natural antagonists in ships, it must be considered that, upon the whole, the Monitor principle contains the most successful elements for plating vessels for war purposes.

"I have the honor to be, very respectfully, your obedient servant,

"JOHN RODGERS, *Commodore U. S. N.*
"Hon. GIDEON WELLES, *Secretary of the Navy.*"

The importance of these statements from experienced naval officers, who have been eye-witnesses of the performance of the Monitors, and the effect of the shot of the fifteen-inch guns, cannot be overrated. They seem to insure our nation from foreign attack, at least, until great changes are made in naval war. · No ship of the broadside class, Commodore Rodgers thinks, can carry a fifteen-inch gun safely, while the Monitors do carry them; and one well-directed shot from one of these guns, he says, would sink any broadside vessel, even the last and most powerful ones of England or France.

Every American should reflect upon the bearing which these facts have upon the future of our nation. It is proved, beyond dispute, that we can build vessels of the Monitor class which can traverse, safely, the whole American coast, which no artillery carried on a broadside ship can penetrate, while the cannon which a Monitor can carry, and with which even our small Monitors are armed, can sink any broadside ship that floats.

The fleets of France and England cannot, therefore, approach our coasts without almost certain destruction. Such a ship as the Dictator, or the Puritan, according to the opinions stated by these eminent officers, would be able to destroy the whole iron-clad navies of France and England, if their ships could be encountered singly, and the only danger from a squadron would be that of being run down. The solution of a mathematical problem is not more certain than that even such a Monitor as the Catawba, now lately launched at Cincinnati, would destroy any ship in the British or French navy, unless (a thing most improbable) she could be run down before she could use her guns. The side-armor of the Catawba, a ship of about eleven hundred tons, is equal to ten inches of solid iron on the hull above the water-line, while her turret is eleven inches thick, and she is, therefore, absolutely invulnerable to any artillery which a broadside ship can carry.

The Government, then, has acted most wisely in adopting the Monitors for its present need. They have secured the nation against foreign attack; and rendered it certain that, within the lines defended by these impregnable floating batteries, we can safely develop our national life, free from all external danger.